SERMONS ON THE
LORD'S PRAYER
AND OTHER PRAYERS OF JESUS

BOOKS BY THE SAME AUTHOR

SERMONS ON THE LORD'S PRAYER
AND OTHER PRAYERS OF JESUS

CLOVIS G. CHAPPELL

ABINGDON PRESS
NEW YORK • NASHVILLE

SERMONS ON THE LORD'S PRAYER

Copyright MCMXXXIV by Whitmore & Smith

M

SET UP, PRINTED, AND BOUND BY THE
PARTHENON PRESS, AT NASHVILLE,
TENNESSEE, UNITED STATES OF AMERICA

CONTENTS

5

SERMONS ON THE LORD'S PRAYER

PART III

A PRAYER OF THANKSGIVING

PART IV

JESUS PRAYING WITH HIS DISCIPLES

PART I
INTRODUCTORY MESSAGE

I

JESUS A MAN OF PRAYER
"He was praying in a certain place."
LUKE 11: 1

IT IS MY PURPOSE TO STUDY WITH YOU DURING THE
next few weeks some of the prayers of our Lord. I
am doing this because I am convinced that very few of
us are making of prayer what it is our privilege to
make. In fact, I fear that there are many, even in our
churches, for whom prayer as a working force is a
lost art. Some of these have been silenced, perhaps,
because of intellectual difficulties. There are others
who have given up prayer because of moral difficulties.
In the secret place they have been brought face to
face with surrenders that they were unwilling to make.
When called upon to give up self, or to give up prayer,
they have given up the latter. But by far the greatest
number of those who have ceased to pray have done so,
I am sure, through no definite conviction of the futility of prayer. They have, rather, drifted into the habit
of prayerlessness by allowing the prayer-hour to be
crowded out by duties that seemed more pressing and
more rewarding. In view of these conditions, there-

9

fore, it seems to me altogether wise for us to consider something of what Jesus teaches about this important matter.

I

As a beginning, and somewhat by way of introduction, we are going to study together to-day the place of prayer in the life of our Lord. Just what did Jesus make of prayer? As we turn the pages of the New Testament we cannot shut our eyes to the fact that he made much of it. This we say, not because he ever argued at length on the subject. He never sought to prove the reality and efficacy of prayer by cold logic any more than he sought to prove the reality of God. He did something infinitely more helpful and impressive. He practiced prayer. He demonstrated its worth by making constant use of it. He literally fulfilled the wise admonition that Paul in later years gave to his converts: "He prayed without ceasing."

At the beginning of his ministry, as he came up from the waters of baptism, it was as he was praying that the heavens were opened, and that the Spirit of God came upon him. Therefore, when in later days he said to his disciples, "If ye, being evil, know how to give good gifts unto your children, how much more shall your Father in heaven give the Holy Spirit to them that ask him," he was speaking out of his own experience. Prayer marks the entire course of his ministry. His whole life was lived in constant communion with God. When he was at the end of the way, his very latest breath was a prayer, "Father, into thy hands I commend my spirit."

II

How did Jesus pray? He laid down no hard and fast rules. But as we study his habit of prayer, we find these characteristics:

1. Jesus constantly addresses God as "Father." Only in his hour of darkness on the cross does he vary from this fixed custom. Here he makes the words of one of the psalmists his own, and cries, "My God, my God, why hast thou forsaken me?" But everywhere else he calls God "Father." There are never any words of endearment. Sometimes he says, "Holy Father," or "Righteous Father," but he never employs "dear" or "loving," as we sometimes do. He felt that the one word "Father" was rich and deep enough without any qualifying adjective. It ought to be for ourselves. To try to add to that is as futile as spraying a honeysuckle with cheap perfume, or undertaking to enhance the beauty of a landscape of snow by sprinkling it with talcum powder.

2. Where did Jesus pray? The answer is, Everywhere. He prayed with his disciples. He had family prayer with them as our fathers used to do with us. He prayed with them in lesser groups. One day he went into a mountain to pray, and took with him Peter and James and John. It was as he prayed in this little company that he was transfigured just as men are

transfigured to-day who pray as he prayed. Then, Jesus prayed alone. The record would seem to indicate that the seasons of prayer that cost him most in time and energy were those that he spent alone in the mountains or elsewhere with his Father.

3. If we ask when Jesus prayed, we must answer that he prayed without ceasing. But he gave himself with peculiar earnestness to prayer at all times of crisis. For instance, when the time was at hand for him to choose the Twelve; when he had to select from among those who were His followers the men upon whose shoulders, in a peculiar sense, he was to place the responsibilities of his Church, he felt the need of Divine guidance. Therefore, he went apart to pray. And we read that he spent the entire night in prayer. Again in the garden, as he faced the cross, while his disciples slept their way to inevitable defeat, he prayed his way toward victory.

But not only did Jesus pray as he faced a coming conflict, but he prayed with equal diligence after the battle was won. Here is where we so often fail. There are many of us who pray after a fashion when we find ourselves in sore straits. But when we have won through, when deliverance has come, then we cease to pray. Thus, we often change our successes into failure; and our bright mornings into blackest night. Jesus never blundered after this fashion. In the first chapter of the Gospel according to St. Mark, we read of a thrillingly victorious day that he spent in

Capernaum. All day long he taught and healed and gave himself without stint to the needy souls about him. Then, the closing hour brought his labors to a fitting climax. "At even, when the sun did set, they brought unto him all that were diseased, and them that were possessed with demons. And all the city was gathered together at the door. And he healed many that were sick with divers diseases, and cast out many demons." And when he went to Simon's house that night, he doubtless lay down wearily to rest with the consciousness of work well done. But he did not allow his victory to make him careless. He rather made of it a stepping stone to a large victory by the fact that, "In the morning, rising up a great while before day, he went out, and departed into a solitary place, and there prayed."

On another occasion he decided to go with his disciples for a picnic on the shores of Galilee. They had all been exceedingly busy and were a bit weary. But the people learned of this proposed retirement, and the keel of the Master's boat had not touched the sand of the shore before the multitudes began to gather. Jesus forgot his needed rest, and gave his entire day to teaching and healing. When the disciples desired to send the multitudes away to get themselves food, he spread for them a table. At last, toward nightfall, he dismissed them. Then, we read, "When he had sent the multitudes away, he went up into a mountain apart to pray; and when the evening was come, he was

13

alone." And it was there that he found spiritual refreshment for himself. It was there that he made the victory of the day a foundation for a greater victory to-morrow.

4. When we inquire as to the objects for which Jesus prayed, we find that he prayed concerning all the needs and the interests of his life. He prayed for himself. He called over the longings of his own heart before God. He prayed for his disciples as a group. He prayed for all who should believe on him through their word. That is, he prayed for the Church of yesterday, and to-day and to-morrow. He prayed for his disciples individually. Luke tells us that it was after he had been praying alone that he asked his disciples, "Who do men say that I am?" And when Peter answered, "Thou art the Christ, the Son of the living God," Jesus cried with joyful enthusiasm, "Flesh and blood hath not revealed this unto thee, but my Father which is in heaven." And the context would indicate that Peter received his revelation in answer to the prayer of Jesus. On another occasion he said to Peter specifically, "I have prayed for thee that thy faith fail not!" Thus Jesus calleth his own sheep by name, not only to lead them out, but to bring their individual needs before his Father and ours.

5. Finally, Jesus put prayer first. He made it central. He did not consider prayer as so many of us do—as a mere preparation for the battle. He considered it the battle itself. It is George Adams Smith

who calls our attention to this fact. It was in the
secret place that Jesus won the fight. It was on his
knees that he gained the victory. All else was little
more than the going forth of a conqueror to receive
the spoils of conquest. Not long ago I had the privilege
of being present at a commencement occasion. The
master of ceremonies called a certain young chap forward and presented him with a medal for having made
the highest grade in the graduating class. There was
no mark of present conflict or strain on the young
fellow's face as he came forward. In fact, I might
have turned to the friend sitting beside me and said,
"How dead easy it is to win a scholarship medal.
Why, all that fellow had to do was simply to walk
across the platform and reach forth his hand." But,
had I made such a remark, my friend would doubtless have reminded me that this medal was not won on
commencement day. It had been won through days
and nights of toil stretching away into the months.
Thus did Jesus win his fight in the secret place of
prayer, and the Father who seeth in secret rewarded
him openly.

III

Now, to be convinced that prayer was the real field
of battle with Jesus, it is only necessary to glance again
at the record. There were times when Jesus worked
with poise and with no seeming strain. But there were
other times when he was obviously putting forth tre-

mendous effort. There were times when he was engaged in a conflict that was intense. There were times
when the battles that he fought were so desperate as
to mean absolute agony. Once at least, we see him in
such a terrible struggle that his sweat was as great
drops of blood falling down to the ground. When
were these desperate hours? They were not, as we
would naturally suppose, those days of dealing with
the great multitudes, friendly and unfriendly, that so
constantly surrounded him. They were his hours of
prayer. If we take the New Testament as our guide,
we are driven to the conclusion that the only work that
ever really taxed the energies of Jesus was the work of
prayer. Having won here, all else seems to have been
accomplished with consummate ease.

Take, for instance, the matter of his dealing with
his enemies. Hostile crowds constantly dogged his
steps, especially during the latter part of his ministry.
Many of these men were keen and unscrupulous. They
were masters of debate. They were desperately eager
to rob him of his poise, and thus entrap him into saying
some foolish or discrediting word. But all their efforts
were in vain. In the most heated argument he never
let fall a single syllable that he had to take back, or
amend in the slightest degree. No question, however
keen, ever took him by surprise. When his foes were
most certain that they had him, he flashed a devastating
answer that left them looking foolish.

One day, for example, they came with this question:

"Is it lawful to give tribute to Cæsar?" How shrewd! It is a question that demands a "yes" or a "no." If Jesus answers "yes," then every respectable Jew will hate him. If he answers "no," then Rome's iron hand will grip and destroy him. If he escapes Scylla, he will surely fall into a Charybdis. But Jesus walked through their well-set trap as easily as a giant would break a gossamer thread. "Show me a penny," he requests. And they put a coin in his hand. "Whose is the image and superscription?" "Cæsar's," is the prompt reply. "Then," said Jesus quietly, "render unto Cæsar the things that are Cæsar's, and to God the things that are God's." And they fairly gasped with amazement. And we are not surprised when we read, "And no man after that durst ask him any question."

Then, see him in the midst of his works of wonder. A leper flings himself at his feet with the prayer, "Lord, if thou wilt, thou canst make me clean." "I will," is the reply; "be thou clean." How easy it looks! On another day a father comes, bringing his afflicted boy. Jesus is away at the time. But his disciples undertake the task of curing the lad, only to fumble it miserably. A little later, when Jesus comes upon the scene, he finds his disciples in utter confusion. They are the laughingstock of their foes. And the father is on the verge of despair because they, by their failure, have shattered his faith. But Jesus is at once master of the situation. He changes failure into success, and defeat into victory. When it is all over, these chastened disciples come to Jesus with one of the wisest questions they ever asked: "Why could not we cast them out?" "We tried," they seemed to say, "just as genuinely as you did." "Your failure," Jesus answers, "was not your lack of effort on the day of the battle; it was your lack of prayer before the battle. This kind can come forth by nothing but prayer."

Again we are amazed with what serene confidence Jesus stands by the grave of Lazarus. Martha is kind enough to remind him that the deceased has now been dead four days, and that, therefore, the situation is totally beyond hope. But, Jesus is not disturbed in the least. Standing by that tomb, he does not ask in agony that God restore Lazarus to life. He rather utters a brief prayer of thanksgiving; "Father, I thank thee that thou hearest me always." And then, with an authority that the dead cannot resist, he cries, "Lazarus, come forth!" Jesus did not win his victory at that grave. He won it in the secret place. It was on the way there that he groaned in spirit and troubled himself. Therefore, having won at prayer, the actual raising of the dead was only the victor receiving the spoils of his conquest.

The same confident poise marks him during the ordeal of the cross. Had I been in the garden of Gethsemane on that Thursday evening long ago, and seen Jesus on his face before God; had I heard him as, in agony, he poured forth his supplication with strong crying and tears, I should doubtless have regarded him with great misgivings. "Surely," I should have said, "if he is thus shaken when alone with his friends, how utter will be his collapse when his enemies come upon him. If he is so broken at the mere prospect of the cross, how completely must he be overwhelmed when he meets its grim horror face to face!"

Then, in the distance, I hear the tramp of many feet, and the hum of many voices. The soldiers and the mob have come at last. "Whom seek ye?" asks a voice of authority. "Jesus of Nazareth," is the answer. "I am he," is the calm reply. And the man who a little while ago seemed utterly shattered steps forward with such poise and kingly majesty that John tells us that these sturdy soldiers must needs stagger back and fall to the ground. And when a little later he stands in the presence of Pilate, it is the Governor that is afraid and not the prisoner. "Art thou a king?" Pilate questions. "Sayest thou this thing of thyself," Jesus replies, "or did others tell it thee of me?" Pilate, are you speaking out of your own experience, or from heresay? Am I your King? Then he continues: "I am a King. To this end was I born, and for this cause came I into the world, that I should bear witness unto the truth. Pilate, I am a King in the realm of the truth." And before this defenseless and unfriended King, Pilate, the representative of Imperial Rome, is strangely perturbed and unmanned.

At last Jesus hangs upon the cross. But there is still a moral and spiritual kingliness about him that at least one of the robbers who is hanging at his side cannot resist. The revilings of his companion in crime become unbearable. "Dost not thou fear God," he flings at him, "seeing thou art in the same condemnation? And we indeed justly; but this man hath done nothing amiss." And then he turns to Christ with this amazing prayer, "Jesus, remember me when thou comest in thy kingdom." "I know," he seems to say, "that thou art a King. I have penetrated thy disguise of nakedness, and shame, and death, and have seen thee for what thou art. So, remember me when thou comest in thy kingdom." And this dying Christ answers with perfect assurance: "Today wilt thou be with me in paradise." Surely if "Socrates died like a philosopher, Jesus Christ died like a God." And everywhere his victory was won in the secret place of prayer.

IV

Now, if prayer was central in the life of our Lord, it ought to be so in your life and mine. If Jesus won his battles in the secret place, where ought we to expect to win ours? If his times of stress and strain were when he was upon his knees, when are yours and mine? He agonized in the closet, but walked with the stride of a conqueror when he went forth into the outer world. Too often we take our ease in the closet, and then go forth to defeat and failure. With sorrow and humility we must confess that we are often far more like those hot and flustered disciples of the long ago,

who stood powerless in the presence of the demands
made upon them, than we are like our victorious Lord.
Yet, prayer is as truly the privilege of ourselves as it
was of Jesus. Our trouble is that we have not learned
what he is trying so hard to teach us, and that is, that
to win in the place of prayer is to win everywhere;
and to fail there is, in some measure, to fail everywhere.

To be convinced of this it is only necessary, if we
have ever really prayed, to consult our own experiences.
When have been our times of failure? When have we
won the victory? Most of us can answer these questions in terms of prayer. Some years ago I was sent
to a certain village to serve a church that was little
more than a wreck. My predecessor, a very popular
man, had been forced, under a cloud, to leave the ministry and membership of the Church. As a result, the
congregation was divided, and the church greatly dis-
credited. After looking the situation over, I decided
that a real spiritual awakening was our one hope. I
undertook to do the preaching, but invited to assist
me a certain layman whom I knew to be mighty in
prayer. For ten days we labored, seemingly in vain.
On the tenth night this brother came with radiant face
to tell me of the coming victory. I shall never forget
the service that followed. It marked the beginning
of a new day in that church and, to some extent, in
the entire community. But the real battle was won in
advance. All we did in the actual service was to gather

the spoils that had been won in the place of prayer.
It is ever so. Therefore, let us highly resolve to strive
to give prayer the place in our lives that it had in
the life of him whom we confess as our Lord and
Master.

PART II
THE MODEL PRAYER

II

PRAY AS SONS

"After this manner therefore pray ye: Our Father which art in heaven."

MATTHEW 6: 9

❋

WE ARE BEGINNING TO-DAY A STUDY OF THAT matchless gem of the devotional life called "The Lord's Prayer." This is one of our Lord's choicest lessons in the high art of prayer. It was not, however, his first lesson. He taught his disciples their first lesson in prayer by his own practice of prayer. That which first awakened in their hearts a desire to pray was not what he said about prayer, but what he did about it. That is always the most effective and convincing method of teaching. If my friend desires instruction on as simple a matter as the correct way of tying his tie, I am likely to show him how it is done rather than merely explain the matter to him. Precepts are helpful when they are used to supplement practice. But lectures alone are of little worth. It is useless, for instance, to enjoin kindness if we ourselves are not kind. Likewise lectures on prayer are of small

25

value if we ourselves do not pray. Jesus had many sharp things to say about the Pharisees, but nothing sharper than when he told the multitude to obey their precepts, but not to imitate their conduct.

It was through his own prayer-life that Jesus brought his disciples to the realization of their past failure in prayer. As they watched him pray, it came home to them how pitifully inadequate their own praying had been. Against the white background of his victorious communion with God, they saw something of the emptiness and futility of their own. But the example of Jesus did far more for them than that. As they saw him at prayer, they not only became convinced of their own past failures, but also of their amazing possibilities. As they beheld him upon his knees, they could not but say to themselves: "That is the way we ought to pray. And by the grace of God, it is the way in which we can pray, once we have learned the secret." So they came to Jesus wistfully and hopefully with this wise request, "Lord, teach us to pray. Though we missed the way yesterday, we are sure we can find it under thy guidance to-day and to-morrow."

And I am hoping that some such holy ambition may lay hold upon our hearts as we take our place at the feet of Jesus in the study of this prayer. God, grant that this may be the case. For I am convinced that about the greatest weakness of the modern Church is to be found in the paltriness of its prayer-life. We are well equipped in many directions. We have the best-trained ministry the Church has ever known, and that is good. We have the best-trained teaching force in our Church schools. We have the best physical equipment for the carrying on of our work of any generation so far. But somehow the work lags, and our efforts are often disappointing. Sometimes they seem as futile as those of a shorn Samson. What is the matter? Maybe practical James gives the answer when he says: "You have not, because you do not pray." A prayerless church is a powerless church. Withheld prayer is a sin. "God forbid that I should sin against the Lord in ceasing to pray for you."

It is heartening, therefore, to remember that when these disciples came with this wise request, Jesus did not rebuke them. He did not turn them away. He taught them to pray. He taught them by giving them this form of prayer. There are those who are constantly reminding us that this is the disciple's prayer rather than the Lord's prayer. But it is both his and ours. There is one petition, of course, that Jesus did not pray, and that is for the forgiveness of sins. But the other petitions were his as they are to be ours. In fact this prayer gives us a deep insight into the mind and heart of our Master. Here we find his conception of God. Here we find those values that he thought most worth living for and most worth dying for. Here we find his dearest hopes and dreams. Here we see the faith that steadied him and enabled him to tread the wine press alone. Jesus lived this prayer. It was wrought out in his life before it became articulate upon his lips. And he is eager to share its treasures with you and me.

It is encouraging, too, to remember that these faulty disciples did finally learn how to pray. There came a time when they could make this prayer their very own. And that is about the highest human achievement. Of course there were many failures. Once when a desperate father brought his son to be cured, they fumbled the task miserably, changed their opportunity into scorn from their enemies, humiliation for themselves, and despair for the one whom they were seeking to help. When Jesus came on the scene and brought victory out of defeat, he told them that the reason for their failure was their lack of prayer. Then there came another day when the skies were full of clouds and they faced other opportunities that threatened to become big impossibilities. But they had in some measure learned their lesson. They betook themselves to prayer, and their weakness became strength and their bewilderment became wisdom. "When they had prayed, the place was shaken where they were assembled together, and they were all filled with the Holy Spirit."

Now there may be those who will have to stifle a yawn at the mere thought of listening to a series of sermons on this familiar subject. There is doubtless not a single soul present who cannot quote this prayer from memory. You can say it while thinking of something else. You can say it while looking back upon yesterday or forward to to-morrow. This may kill your interest. I undertook to show a friend a beautiful building sometime ago, but he passed it by without a glance, merely saying, "I have seen it before." Familiarity often hangs a veil over the face of the beautiful. The stars were out last night, but you did not take time to look up into their silvery eyes because you had seen them before. There was a miracle of a sunrise this morning, but it had not a glance from you. You had seen the sun rise before. Even the tender ministries of love, the hug of baby arms, the handclasp of friends that were yours this morning brought little thrill. You have become so accustomed to them that you take them as a matter of course. Thus some, perchance, will face these priceless gems that make up the Lord's Prayer, and pass them by with sightless eyes, saying only, "I have seen them before."

But I am sure that there are others for whom familiarity has bred, not contempt, but a deeper love. Though you have heard, and though you have prayed this prayer countless numbers of times, yet, instead of losing its appeal it has grown more precious with the passing of the years. You have prayed it with the tender lips of childhood. You have prayed it in the intimacy of the family circle. You have prayed it in the great congregation. You have prayed it in times of joy, and you have prayed it when you were so sorely wounded that you could not find any words of your own to express your deep needs. But to-day it is more dear, more amazingly priceless than ever before

And then it may quicken our interest as we make this study to think how many have prayed it before us, and how many are praying it with us even now. What multitudes, as the centuries have come and gone, have found this prayer a vehicle upon which their souls have been carried up to God, as Elijah upon his chariot of fire! It has been prayed by white-souled men and women as they struggled in the thick of the battle of life. It has been prayed by the prisoner in his cell, by the condemned man upon the scaffold. It has been prayed by the mightiest of saints. It has also been upon the lips of the pathetic outcast who, like the publican, dared not lift up his eyes to heaven. It has been prayed by millions who are now in that miracle country where prayer has given place to praise. It is being prayed by unknown multitudes that walk our earth to-day. Let us join our voices with theirs!

I

The first lesson that Jesus teaches us in this prayer is a right conception of the One to whom we pray. The importance of this is evident at once. Our conception of the One to whom we pray will surely determine both the nature and expectancy of our prayers. It is possible to think of God in such a way as to make real prayer an impossibility. Years ago, while

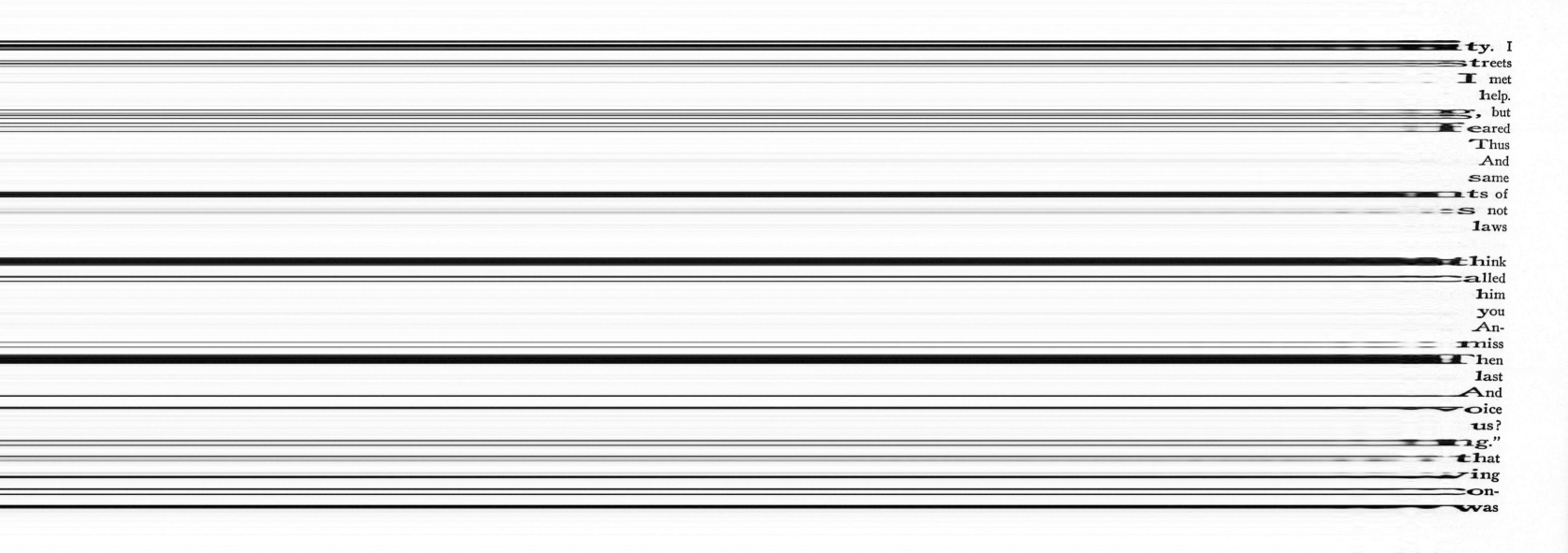

true in the begin
end. When he
Father, if it be
Only once in si
endearing term
darkness on the
God, why hast t
passed, and at t
arms as a tire
saying, "Father
"When ye pr
for everybody
world that cann
all creeds. It i
far into the he
prayer, also, fo
realization that
for the holy n
pious and pure
a prayer, also,
self away, and
sel of bread.
is the Father
Not only is
heaven. By s
mean to locate
lives. Those
only, usually t
how we have

way off. That conception has crept into many of our songs. "There is a happy land, far, far away." And even in that popular hymn, "The Old Rugged Cross," we sing, "He will call me some day to that home far away." How did we get that conception? Certainly not from the New Testament. When Jesus was talking to Nicodemus, he said, "No man hath ascended up to heaven, but he that came down from heaven, even the Son of man who is in heaven." That is, Jesus claimed that while he was sitting and talking to this rabbi, he himself was actually in heaven. This means, of course, that heaven is here and now. I can believe in a heaven for to-morrow, because I have known some of its joys in yesterday. And I can believe in hell for the same reason. If this, therefore, were intended to locate God, as it is not, it would mean that he is very near.

When Jesus says, "Our Father who art in heaven," he is describing God. Heaven is the place of perfection. He is telling us, therefore, that God is not only our Father, but that he is the perfect Father. The appeal of the word "father" depends upon the pictures that it brings to your mind, the memories that it stirs. It is not a beautiful word to everybody. To some it suggests one who was selfish and unloving and unlovable. Or worse still, it recalls one who stole the roses from your mother's cheek, robbed you of your childish joys, and made a hell of what might have been a home. But that is not true of all of us, thank God! When I

33

hear the word I look into eyes that were keen and kind and unafraid. I see a face strong and pure and tender. I think of one who lived not for himself, but for others, who offered himself as a daily sacrifice for the service of those he loved. I think of one who could be stern at times, but who could also be as gentle as a mother. I remember one night as a lad, when it was thought that I could not live till morning. It was Father who came to tell me about it, and to help me to face it unafraid. It was he that undertook, the best he could, to gather me into his fatherly arms, and to hand me into the arms of that infinite Father from whom every family in heaven and earth takes its name.

And Jesus said, "Take fatherhood at its best and lift it unto the realm of the infinite, and you will have some conception of God." He is our heavenly Father. He is perfect in his knowledge of us. He knows what we need before we ask him. Because he knows, he sometimes has to refuse our foolish and selfish requests. He is perfect in his love, infinitely eager to answer our prayers. That has been said countless times before, yet most of us still do not believe it. We are convinced, though we hardly dare put it into words, that God could do a lot more for us than he is doing. That is what the leper thought. Poor fellow, life had dealt harshly with him. He had been rebuffed and disappointed so many times that he did not believe that there was any such thing in the world as love. So, when he flung himself down at the feet of Jesus, he said, "Lord, if thou wilt, thou canst make me clean. I believe you have the power, but I am not convinced that you care." But Jesus said, "I do care." And he touched him unto purity. God is also perfect in his ability. Sometimes we face situations where we would give our very lives to help, but we cannot. But if we give him a chance, it is never the case with God. "Lord," we sometimes cry with that desperate father who brought his son to Jesus, "Lord, if thou canst do anything, have mercy upon us and help us." "You have put the 'if' at the wrong place," Jesus said. "If thou canst believe, all things are possible to him that believeth." He is our perfect Father.

II

Now since God is our Father, we are to take the position of sons. I said awhile ago that God is the Father of all of us. Therefore, we are his children. But all are not children in the same sense. Broadly speaking, God's children are divided into two groups: Those who recognize their sonship and enter into the enjoyment of it, and those who do not; those who claim their birthright, and those who disinherit themselves. Jesus said to certain Pharisees who had just claimed sonship to God, "You are of your father the devil." They were sons by creation and by right, but they were not claiming their birthright. But the Apostle John declares, "As many as received him, to them gave he power to become the sons of God." And he has claimed his rights and has taken the position of a son. Therefore, we hear his joyful shout across the far spaces of the years, "Behold, what manner of love the Father hath bestowed upon us, that we should be called the sons of God."

Jesus told the story of a certain laddie who played in both rôles. This boy became tormented by the mad dream that he would find life fuller and more joyous away from his father's presence. Therefore, he said to his father, "Give me the portion of goods that falleth to me. . . . And not many days after he gathered all together, and took his journey into a far country, and there wasted his substance with riotous living. And when he had spent all . . . he began to be in want. And he went and joined himself to a citizen of that country; and he sent him into his fields to feed swine. And he would fain have filled himself with the husks that the swine did eat: and no man gave unto him." But hungry and destitute as he was, he was still his father's son, and that father still loved him, and longed with infinite yearning for him to come back home and claim his birthright.

Then one day this son, who had disinherited himself, who had looted his own safe and flung away his own treasure, came to himself. He began to be haunted by the tender memories of a better day, to be wooed by an appealing love that would not let him go. At last he could resist no longer. He said, "I will arise and go"—not out of this pigsty, not even home, but—

PRAY AS SONS

"I will arise and go to my father. . . . And he arose, and came to his father. But when he was yet a great way off, his father saw him, and had compassion, and ran, and fell on his neck, and kissed him . . . and said, Bring forth the best robe, and put it on him; and put a ring on his hand, and shoes on his feet." Thus he gave him, not the place of a servant, but the place of a son. And to all such, prayer is as natural and inevitable as the love of a child for its mother. For, "because ye are sons, God hath sent forth the Spirit of his Son into your hearts, crying, Father!"

37

III

PRAY AS BROTHERS

"After this manner therefore pray ye: Our Father."

MATTHEW 6: 9

IN MY INTRODUCTORY MESSAGE I CONFINED MYSELF to the address of the Lord's Prayer, "Our Father who art in heaven." I tried to give emphasis to two of the lessons that Jesus teaches us from this address. First, we are to think of God as he thought of him, as our Father. He is the Father of all mankind, high and low, rich and poor together. Not only so, but he is our heavenly Father. That means that he is our perfect Father. He is perfect in his knowledge of us. He knows what we need before we ask him. He is perfect in his love toward us. He is perfect in his ability to help us. The second lesson we tried to emphasize was that, since he is our Father, we ought to take the positions of sons.

Now it is a great privilege to be a son of God. It ought to make a fretful and feverish attitude toward life impossible. It ought to enable us to face whatever comes of joy or sorrow with quiet hearts and steady eyes. But if we take the positions of sons, there is something more involved than privilege. There is also obligation. If we pray as sons, we must also pray as brothers. To do that brings life's finest crown, but it brings crucifixion first. It is easy to confess our faith in the brotherhood of man, but to live as a brother is not so easy. This is a prayer, therefore, as another has said, "that takes away our cushions and leaves us a cross."

I

When Jesus taught us to pray after this fashion, he was cherishing the maddest and the most amazingly beautiful dream of which the human heart can conceive. He was looking forward to a good day when all self-seeking and oppression and unbrotherly competition should be done away. He was looking forward to a time when the wide chasms that separate man from man, and nation from nation, and race from race should be no more. He was dreaming of a time when the song of peace and good will that the angels sang above the starlit heights of Bethlehem should become a radiant reality. For he is here to gather together into one the sons of God that are scattered abroad. The madness of this dream can be readily realized in the light of the day in which Jesus lived. He was a part of a little conquered nation at the back side of the Roman Empire. Rome's grim eagles held the world of that day in their iron claws. Political oppression was everywhere. More than half the population of the empire was in actual slavery. Cruelty and injustice stalked abroad. Right was trodden under foot of might and splendor rode hard on the bony shoulders of squalor. Yet this daring Man prayed and taught us to pray for a time when all these evils should be done away, and men should brothers be all round the world.

Now much progress has been made since that far-off time. The heart of humanity, thanks to the spirit of brotherhood released by Jesus, has become far more kind and tender. More men are thinking in terms of world peace and of brotherhood to-day than ever before. But while thanking God for this progress, we cannot shut our eyes to the fact that the dream of Jesus is yet unmeasured distances from realization. Though it is his purpose to gather us together into one, though he longs that there shall be one flock and one Shepherd, yet as we look abroad, we cannot shut our eyes to the fact that, instead of oneness, there is division everywhere.

1. There is division in the heart of the individual. Multitudes have lost all sense of God. The man who is without God is at war with himself. "There is no peace, saith my God, unto the wicked." The tragedy of this inner strife has sobbed its way through the centuries. Here is a prayer of an ancient Psalmist, "My soul cleaveth unto the dust: quicken thou me." He is conscious of a hunger for God. But while with

one hand he feels out after God, with the other he is reaching after mud and muck. He is, therefore, divided within himself. "Unite my heart to fear thy name," pleads another of these ancient saints. And here is a cry from the lips of St. Paul that has been voiced by countless millions, "O wretched man that I am! who shall deliver me?" Deliver him from what? From the tragedy of a divided self. On every hand to-day we find men who are at war with themselves.

2. There is also division between man and man. This division we often find in groups that are the most intimate. There is division within the family. The nearer we are together, the more intensely we can hate. There is division within our clubs and fraternities; division even within our churches. How difficult it is to get people to live together as brothers! The early church has hardly been welded into a brotherhood by the outpouring of the Holy Spirit till we begin to hear distressing notes of discord. "There arose a murmuring." That is a familiar sound. Sad to say we often hear it even in the family of God. We ought never to cease to deplore the tragedy of the divisions in the body of Christ. Even we who are Methodists have not yet succeeded in getting together.

3. Then, think of the wide chasms that separate nation from nation. We said a moment ago that more people were thinking in terms of world peace to-day than ever before. Yet while we talk peace, we make frantic preparations for war. Our own government

is spending hundreds of millions of dollars in these days of depression for machines whose sole purpose is the shedding of blood. We have realized something of the devilish deadliness of war. But that is not enough. The nations must become brotherly. And that is not their attitude at this hour. The only reason some of our leading nations are not fighting now is because they are economically unable. The words of our Master are tragically true here: "The spirit indeed is willing, but the flesh is weak."

II

How are these divisions to be healed? How did our Lord set about healing them in his day?

He did not do so by tampering with superficialities. He did not look to mere external organization to bring this about. When Ezekiel went into that valley of death, he found nothing but disintegrating bones. When he left, those bones had been transformed into an exceedingly great army. That is, they were not only alive, but they were united. They were more than a mob. They had been made one by their loyalty to a common leader. How was this brought to pass? Not by polishing a few individual bones, not by tying together a few skeletons. The remedy had to go deeper than that. They had been made one because the breath of God had breathed upon them.

Even so, when Jesus set about the gigantic task of making the world into a brotherhood, he went to the heart of things. He sought to gather about him a few men that he could build into a brotherhood. The task looked small and narrow. It was distressingly slow and discouraging. Up to the very cross, these fussy friends of his were quarreling among themselves as to who should be greatest. When they came to their last meal together it was Jesus rather than one of themselves who had to take the place of a servant. But he never lost heart, and after he had washed their feet, he gave them his new commandment, "A new commandment I give unto you, That ye love one another."

What is there new about this commandment? The answer is at first surprising and disappointing. It is new, not in its breadth, but in its narrowness. The old commandment is broad, "Thou shall love the Lord thy God with all thy heart . . . and thy neighbor as thyself." That is as wide as the world. It enjoins love for all men. But this new commandment only commands one Christian to love his fellow Christians. It was thus that Jesus sought to unite his followers into a fellowship so close as to make them one family. They were to be a temple built of living stones. They were to be one single body in Christ. They were to be in a true sense what Peter called them—"The Brotherhood." And there is no mistaking the fact that when Jesus taught us to say "Our Father" he meant that we think especially of our fellow Christians. And Paul was but voicing the teaching of his Master when he said, "As we have therefore opportunity, let us do good unto all men, especially unto those who are of the household of faith."

I am aware that to some this will seem very narrow, and we are averse to narrowness. But remember that it is the narrowness of Jesus, and that his narrowness always faces out toward infinite breadth. When he was having family prayer with his disciples for the last time, he said, "I pray not for the world, but for them whom thou hast given me . . . and for those who shall believe on me through their word." And his prayer for these was that they might be one. And what was to be the end of this oneness? Not that they should get out of the world and into heaven. He prayed that they might be one in order that the world might believe. He knew that this world would never be made into a brotherhood by unbrotherly and self-seeking men. It takes brotherly men to build a brotherhood. He believed that the surest way to world-wide conquest was for one Christian to love another. "By this shall all men know that ye are my disciples, if ye have love one to another." And the history of the Church has amply vindicated that faith. What was it, for instance, about the early church that first astonished and bewildered, and then wooed and won? How did this little group of Christians come to conquer the pagan world? It was not their love for all mankind primarily. It was their love for one another. "Look," they said in wistful wonder, "how these Christians love each other." And because they themselves wanted to love and to be

44

loved, because they wanted to get into a homelike atmosphere, because they were eager to live among brothers, they were drawn into these little despised groups that were scattered over the Roman Empire.

Surely this is a lesson that the Church of to-day needs to take to heart. It is a lesson for the individual congregation. It is a lesson for this congregation. As narrow as it may seem, the finest service that you and I can render to our city and to our world is by loving each other. And by loving, I do not mean a mere sentiment, I mean a goodwill that is active and self-forgetful and sacrificial. If our Lord cannot make a brotherhood out of First Methodist Church, how can we ever pray with faith for him to make a brotherhood out of the wide world? If we ourselves do not love our brothers whom we have seen, how can we love those whom we have not seen? If we are to believe in the brotherhood of man, we must see it work in the here and now. But our brotherliness is not vastly impressive. Sad to say, we of this congregation do not even know each other. If we should all go to heaven to-day, the angels would be kept busy for the first few weeks after our arrival introducing us to one another. We sit together without speaking. We often fail to visit the sick of our own church family. We sometimes lose loved ones and allow some fraternity to minister to the bereaved, and thus to take our crown.

Brotherhood means sharing. It means the bearing of one another's burdens. It is useless to say "Our

Father" unless we act like brothers. We have representatives in the foreign field who are part of our brotherhood. Their salaries are pathetically small. Some of them are being starved home because of our unwillingness to share. We have old saints among us who have worn themselves out in our service. They have married us in our youth. They have christened our infants. They have watched by our sick. They have buried our dead. We have drunk up their energies, and now that they are no longer equal to the task we have taken the collar from off their work-worn necks and turned them out on the commons. What an insult to the name of brotherhood is the manner in which we often treat our old superannuated preachers!

These are hard days for the Church. Some churches are actually dying. But there is one church that is certainly going to live, and that is the brotherly church. You simply cannot keep people out of it. A certain man went down from Atlanta to Birmingham and fell among thieves that stripped him and wounded him and departed, leaving him half dead. And by chance the pastor of First Church came that way and saw him and passed by on the other side. Likewise a member of the Official Board came where he was and looked upon him, and passed by on the other side. But a certain man came by who belonged to a heterodox church. He was regarded as a speckled bird. But he took the poor chap to a hospital and had him taken care of. And when the wounded man came round, he repented

of the careless life he had lived, and resolved to join
the Church. But to the amazement of his friends and
to the indignation of the orthodox, he passed by the
fashionable and wealthy and respectable churches of
his city to become a member of the Samaritan Church.
And when his friends asked him why he did it, he answered that he wanted to belong to a church that was
brotherly. Other churches may die. If they do, they
will deserve it. But the brotherly church will live forever, and will go on conquering and to conquer.

III

And let me remind you that this business of being
brotherly is not optional. One day Jesus uttered a
word that brings us all before the judgment seat. This
is what he said, "He that is not for me is against me,
and he that gathereth not with me scattereth abroad."
Here he speaks in harmony with this prayer. His purpose in the world is to unite, to build individual men
into a brotherhood, to gather together in one the sons
of God that are scattered abroad. He divides all men
into two classes—those who stand with him, and those
who oppose him. There is no neutral class. There
are these two and these two only. How are we to distinguish the friends of Jesus from his foes? He himself gives the answer.

1. Who is against Jesus? Every man, he answers,
who tears down, every man who makes for division,
every man who makes it easy to hate and hard to love.

47

I have seen very earnest and well-meaning people who could not pass this test. If you are ready at the least provocation to throw a monkey wrench into the machinery of the Church and cause suspicion and hate between man and man, then you are not a friend of Jesus—you are his enemy. No man who merely tears down can be a disciple of our Lord.

2. Who are his friends? Every man who helps in any way to build up the brotherhood. We are in constant need of building up, both as individuals and as a congregation. "Let everything," wrote Paul, "be done with a view to building." Whoever brings men closer to each other, whoever makes it harder to hate and easier to love, Jesus counts as his friend. A few years ago, a brilliant German named Albert Schweitzer wrote a book called "In Quest of the Historic Jesus." He came to the conclusion that we cannot find the historic Jesus by the pathway of mere scholarship; that, in order to know him, we must obey him. He made up his mind that obedience for him meant being a medical missionary. He chose a field in Equatorial Africa. At the age of thirty he gave up his professorship in the University of Strassburg and took a course in medicine, while his wife took training as a nurse. He then gave concerts, for he is a skilled musician, and the greatest living interpreter of Bach. With the funds thus raised, supplemented by the money received from the sale of his book on Bach, he went out to Africa and established his hospital.

Now a few years later he writes home somewhat after this fashion: "The operation is over, and I am sitting in the dormitory watching the patient, waiting for him to wake. By and by his eyes open, and he ejaculates, 'I have no pain, I have no pain!' Then his hand feels for mine and finds it, and he begins to ask questions. And I tell him and the others who are present that it is the Lord Jesus that told me and my wife to come out to Africa, where there is so much suffering. And as we sit there thus holding hands we know from experience the truth of what Jesus said, 'One is your Master, even Christ, and all ye are brethren.' And I wish that my generous friends at home could live through one such glorious hour." Here we stand face to face with a friend of Jesus. And so are you his friend, if you give even so much as a cup of cold water in his name. For thus you are helping to build up the brotherhood. And to this high task you commit yourself when in prayer you say "Our Father."

IV

PRAY FOR REVERENCE

"Hallowed be thy name."

MATTHEW 6: 9

THIS IS THE FIRST PETITION OF THE LORD'S PRAYER. But while it is first upon our lips when we come to bow before God, I fear that it is the last in our minds and hearts. Even in the holy place of prayer, most of us think first of ourselves and of our own needs. That is one reason that our prayers are so often futile. The first step toward praying aright is to put ourselves in a right attitude toward God. Our first thoughts must be of him. It is, therefore, no arbitrary arrangement that puts this petition first. It comes first, because it is the very gateway into the divine presence. Before we pray for the coming of the kingdom, before we pray for the forgiveness of sins, before we pray for our daily bread, we are to pray that the name of God—that is, that God himself—be hallowed. Our first petition is a prayer for reverence.

I

What do we mean by reverence?

There are those who seem to think of it as mere

50

solemnity. But reverence must go far deeper than
that. One may have a countenance that "creams and
mantles like a standing pool," and yet be very lacking
in this virtue. Jesus knew certain ones in his day who
were accustomed to practice fasting. In order that they
might win due credit for their unwelcome perform-
ances, they made wry faces of deliberate purpose.
They looked as horribly wretched and as grotesquely
solemn as possible. They did this in order that all who
passed them on the street might be compelled to see
how terribly religious they were. But Jesus did not
admire them. He certainly did not look upon them as
models of reverence. He rather thought that the solemnity of their faces was but a blind behind which
they were seeking to hide a flippant, hypocritical, and
irreverent soul.

But while outward solemnity is not reverence, it is,
of course, not necessarily inconsistent with it. One
may be very solemn and very reverent. But one may
also be very sunny and very reverent. For instance,
when we wish to see reverence at its highest and best,
we naturally turn to Jesus. None other was ever so
reverent as he. His whole life was shot through with
that reverent spirit that is born of the conscious presence of God. Yet while he was the most reverent of
men, he was also the most gladsome and sunny. His
gladness, instead of making war against his reverence,
only served to increase it. I should like for my children to have as much reverence for me as their father

as possible. But I should regret very much to learn that what seemed to be reverence was only a caricature that served no higher purpose than to hush their laughter and cause them to be unnaturally solemn in my presence. Reverence, therefore, is by no means a synonym for long-facedness and sour solemnity.

Then there are others who think of reverence as consisting of certain outward forms. It is being silent in church. It is bowing the head and bending the knee. Now I believe that one who is really reverent will do all these. A rosebush cannot have springtime in its heart and keep it a secret. It will proclaim it to the world in terms of color and perfume. I am sure, too, that the springtime of reverence will proclaim its presence by leading its possessor to observe certain outward forms of reverence. I believe, too, that these forms tend to create reverence and to give it a more victorious life. But reverence is something far deeper than any outward form. For it is altogether possible to observe the outward forms of reverence and still be utterly lacking in the reality.

What, then, is reverence? It is an inward something. It is a discerning of the highest and of the best. It is an approval of that which is of real worth. It is the emotion that is stirred within us by whatsoever is lovely and of good report. Of course it is far more than all this. To reverence is to honor. To reverence is to love. It is to love with a love that is not unmixed with fear. When directed toward God, it is all of

52

these—honor, love, and fear—magnified to a superlative degree. It is, therefore, a virtue so immeasurably worthful that there are those who regard it as of supreme worth.

II

Why is reverence so important?

1. It is a mark of character. It indicates a certain fineness of fiber that entitles its owner to a place among the spiritual aristocracy. No man can ever be truly great without it. It is possessed by those, and those only, who have attained some degree of growth in the things of the spirit. We do not expect, for instance, to find this virtue in the very young child. A good many years ago my wife and I introduced our firstborn to a distinguished Judge who was a friend of ours. We did this with typical joy and pride. The Judge, being a most delightful gentleman, undertook to pay the little barbarian some attention. But he, being only some eighteen months of age, did not share the reverence of his parents for this distinguished man of light and learning. In fact, the only reason that he did not slap the good man's face was because he proved to be more skilled in the art of dodging than you would have expected of one in his position.

On another occasion we had in our home a small nephew who had developed the rather ugly habit of saying that he was glad for any misfortune that chanced to befall any one of his companions. One day

53

a splendid old superannuated preacher came to see us. He had served long years in the Christian ministry. He had that hoar head in the way of righteousness that the Scriptures tell us is a crown of glory. He had only one limb, his other having been shot away, I think, on the field of battle. All in all, he was a man for whom we had a profound respect. But this respect was not shared in the least by our young nephew. Therefore, as the old gentleman rose to leave, he danced about him, crying, "I'm glad you haven't got but one leg, I'm glad you haven't got but one leg!" The conduct of both of these little fellows was perfectly outrageous. The only reason we could excuse it at all was because of their extreme youth. But if their attitude never changes, then what? Just this—in a very profound sense, they will forever remain babies, moral and spiritual dwarfs.

Dr. J. K. McClure, to whom I am indebted for more than one helpful suggestion in the preparation of this sermon, tells this story: "One day, while he sat resting in Lincoln Park, Chicago, he saw a splendid gentleman approach the statue of Abraham Lincoln. For a moment this man stood gazing into that rugged face, so full of strength and tenderness, so marked with the deep lines of care. Then he reached up and removed his hat and suffered his white hair to be blown in the wind as he stood uncovered in the presence of the statue of this great and gallant-hearted statesman. Meantime, there was another man sitting on the pedes-

54

tal of the statue, writing obscene verses and staining it with tobacco juice. Now, regardless of what our attitude may be to Abraham Lincoln, whether we honor him as he so justly deserves to be honored, or not, we must realize that there is a difference between these two men that is wider than the spaces between the stars. While one has a certain bigness about him that commands our respect, the other has obviously stamped upon him the mark of the spiritual pigmy.

2. Then, reverence is the gateway to knowledge. This is true in the realm of science. Nature, as another has said, does not disclose her secrets to the man who merely shouts irreverently, "Stand and deliver!" The greatest of the scientists have been men of humility and reverence. Agassiz had this as his motto: "A laboratory is a sanctuary where nothing profane should be allowed to enter." It is to men of this type that nature reveals her amazing secrets. In the presence of the proud, the flippant, the irreverent, she lapses into utter silence.

If this is true in the realm of nature, it is certainly no less true in the realm of the spiritual. We do not find our way into the secret place of the Most High upon flippant and irreverent feet. The man who undertakes to approach God in the attitude of "Hail fellow well met" will miss him altogether. "Moses, Moses, draw not nigh hither: put off thy shoes from off thy feet, for the place whereon thou standest is holy ground." It is the man who is reverent that finds God.

55

It is the soul who is conscious of God that becomes increasingly reverent. In fact, the greater our reverence, the greater our vision; and the clearer our vision, the greater our reverence. These two act and react upon each other.

III

But while recognizing the vast importance of reverence, we cannot fail to realize that its absence is one of the outstanding characteristics of our day. We are short on many virtues, but in none are we more utterly poverty-stricken than in the virtue of reverence. There is no holy place in most of our lives. He spoke truly who said, "Nothing in this generation wears a halo." Even Irving Cobb declared that if we were to examine the bump of reverence on the head of the modern man, we should find it to be a dent. For vast multitudes of us, there is nothing in heaven or earth, in past or present, to make us wonder and worship. It has even become a fashion to dig up the moral and spiritual kings of yesterday and drag their crowns from their brows, and snatch their scepters from their hands. Why is this? What are some of the foes that have warred against, and so nearly destroyed, our reverence?

1. I think our reverence has been greatly hurt by our too great familiarity with the sordid and the unclean. Our generation seems to be obsessed by matters of sex. Now I am not arguing for prudishness. I am not try-

ing to turn back the clock to that day when all sex matters were taboo. But much of our teaching on this delicate question is at best simply vile, damaging, and damning. Many of our books are little less than filthy, and not a few of our pictures glorify the obscene. In the language of Alfred W. Noyes, one-time Poet Laureate of England, "So called art to-day garlands the necks of the Muses with strings of garbage." We have largely lost our capacity to blush. Modesty has fallen dead in the streets. Naturally this easy familiarity with the unclean has made war on our reverence. There is an atmosphere that is so fine and wholesome that it makes it easy for us to wonder and worship. But there is also an atmosphere that is so foul that it makes real reverence next to impossible. There is no measuring the injury that has been done by our too great familiarity with the coarse and common and the unclean.

2. Another foe of reverence is conceit. Sometimes this is the conceit of the self-made man, the man who has made a success of his business. This type is not so numerous as he once was. The depression has killed him off somewhat, but he is not completely exterminated. Jesus introduces us to such a character: "The ground of a certain rich man brought forth plentifully: and he thought within himself, saying, What shall I do, because I have no room where to bestow my fruits? And he said, This will I do: I will pull down my barns, and build greater; and there will I bestow all my fruits

57

and my goods." His whole story is "I—I—I." There is no slightest sense of God, and therefore no reverence. He is just an irreverent fool, slapping himself upon the back with the self-satisfied conviction that if God had not made the world, he would.

Then our reverence is often killed by intellectual conceit. Primitive man lived in a world that filled him with wonder and awe and fear. Every flash of lightning was direct from the hand of Jupiter. The roar of the thunder was the pounding of Thor's heavy hammer. Each tribe had its gods. In addition, there were witches and goblins and ghosts everywhere. Some evil spirit lurked behind every rock or glared from behind every tree. But science has turned her searchlight upon these mysterious creatures, and they have vanished like an evil dream. To-day, we walk with an assured step. We are far too wise to fear anything. Our wonder and awe have gone. Yet, strange to say, we have not solved one single elemental mystery. We are just as completely baffled by the fundamental mysteries of the universe as were our fathers who used to live in the caves and dens of the earth. It is not our wisdom that has killed our reverence, but the opposite. Therefore, Tennyson sings,

> "Let knowledge grow from more to more,
> And more of reverence in us dwell."

3. But the supreme cause of our lack of reverence is our practical atheism. We have lost our sense of God.

As you turn the pages of the Bible, you cannot miss this fact—every man who has a real sense of God in his life is a reverent man. When white-souled Isaiah saw the Lord "high and lifted up," when he heard the seraphim singing, "Holy, holy, holy, is the Lord of hosts," he at once put his lips in the dust with the cry, "Unclean, unclean, unclean!" When John on the Isle of Patmos caught a vision of the risen Lord he said, "I fell at his feet as one dead." He doubtless had some degree of reverence before he ever discovered God, but having found him his reverence grew from more to more.

IV

Now, suppose God answers our prayer this morning! Suppose we come really to hallow his name! What would it mean for us in our daily living? It would mean that we should bring to everything bearing the finger marks of God something of the reverent spirit of Jesus.

1. To reverence God is to have a reverent attitude toward nature. That was true of Jesus. He stood reverently in the presence of the lily of the field. He did this, not simply because of what the lily was in itself, but because God had clothed it. "Earth's crammed with heaven, and every common bush is aflame with God," sings Mrs. Browning. But it is only the reverent that takes off his shoes. The rest sit

around and pick blackberries, and most of us are in the blackberry business.

2. We should share the reverence of Jesus for God's house. Religion was at a low ebb during his days. Once when he came to the temple, his very soul was whipped into a tempest. The voice of worship was drowned by the clank of coins, by the bleating of sheep, by the lowing of cattle, by the shrieks of the money changers, by the howls of the herdsmen. He looked about him with amazement and grief that changed into hot anger. "This is my Father's house," he said. "It is to be a place of prayer. It is to be a place where the soul and God meet face to face and come to understand each other. But you have made it a den of thieves." And in the white-heat of his indignation, he overturned their tables and flung their money upon the floor, and chased them pellmell into the street.

That is an arresting word—"You have made it." It is written, "My house is to be a house of prayer," but "you have made it." Suppose we complete that sentence this morning. What have you made of God's house? Some have turned it over to the bats and spiders. They never come about it. But you, what have you, what are you making of it? Is it a place of worship? Is it a place to which you come reverently? If not, your coming is useless. "Who hath required this at your hands to tread my courts?" We can make God's house a place of reverence, or we can make it a den of thieves where we rob each other of our spiritual treasure. I may cheat you by my own flippancy. The choir may do the same. I have heard choirs sing in a fashion to lift the heart Godward. Then I have known them to sit bolt upright during prayer, to laugh and talk during the sermon, till their fellows were cheated out of an opportunity to worship. We can help each other in God's house, or we can rob each other. If this prayer is answered, we shall help each other, for we shall have a new reverence for the house of God.

3. If this prayer is answered, we shall have a new reverence for the Word of God. We shall come to this Bible with something of the reverent spirit with which Jesus came to his Old Testament. He so reverenced the Bible that he read it. He did not look upon it as a fetish to be carefully taken in hand and dusted off once a week. He did not regard it as a book of wooden rules. He did not consider its every word of equal value. Some parts he corrected, saying, "Ye have heard it was said of old time, . . . but I say unto you." But there were others in which he heard the very voice of God. To these he was constantly turning, and upon these he fed his soul. When men came asking questions, he often answered them from the Bible, instead of out of his own wisdom. Its teachings were his strength in his hours of crisis. They were the swords with which he fought the enemy during his great temptation. They became the vehicle of his agony and aspiration as he hung on the cross.

4. Finally, to have this prayer answered is to share the reverence of Jesus for human personality. He gave us a new estimate of the value of the individual soul. He honored all men. He honored them, not simply for what they were in themselves, but because they were kinsfolk with God. They were made in his image. There were many outcasts in his day. With these, decent folks were forbidden to associate. But Jesus disregarded these prohibitions. He made them his friends and showed that none of them were cast beyond his love and reverence. He honored them so profoundly that in their defense he made himself unpopular, and earned for himself the name of the Friend of publicans and sinners. He honored them so that in his efforts to befriend them he hastened his steps to the cross. Therefore, that we may be Christlike in our reverence, let us pray this prayer: "Hallowed by thy name."

V

PRAY FOR THE KINGDOM

"Thy kingdom come."
MATTHEW 6: 10

❧

THIS PETITION FOR THE COMING OF THE KINGDOM brings us face to face with our Lord's supreme enthusiasm. It is impossible to read the New Testament without realizing that his dearest dream, the one outstanding passion of his heart, was the Kingdom of God. Years before he entered upon his active ministry, he had found this word in his Old Testament. At once it had set the fires of a high and holy expectation to burning in his soul. As he plied his daily task, as he strolled among the solitudes of his native hills, the thought that constantly haunted him and would not let him go was that of the Kingdom of God. It was upon the Kingdom that he meditated as he went to worship at the synagogue. It was of the Kingdom that he spoke to his Father in the secret place of prayer. Doubtless it was often the theme of his conversation with his friends, or as he talked to his mother and to his brothers and sisters in the intimacy of the home circle.

63

At last one day he locked the door of his little shop and left it to return to it no more. He set out to share this supreme enthusiasm with his fellows. When he preached his first sermon, this was his text, "The kingdom of heaven is at hand." And what he said at the beginning, he was constantly saying throughout his ministry. With a genius at which all the centuries have marveled, he told story after story to illustrate the meaning and the supreme worth of the Kingdom. By and by the fires that burned upon the altar of his own heart were kindled within the hearts of a few others. These he sent out to preach. But he did not trust them to select their own theme. He told them that the theme of their preaching was to be the Kingdom of God. It was for the Kingdom he lived. At last it was for the Kingdom that he died. And when he met his disciples again on the resurrection side of the grave, the one passion of his heart had not changed. It was still the Kingdom of God. Luke says that he was seen of them forty days, and that during that time he spake of the things pertaining to the Kingdom of God. No wonder, then, that when he taught his disciples to pray he told them to say, "Thy kingdom come!"

I

For what are we asking when we pray for the coming of the Kingdom? We are asking, of course, that God take the throne of our individual hearts. But we are asking for far more. A kingdom implies subjects.

This is a prayer for others, for a society where the will of God is recognized as supreme. It is a prayer, as another has expressed it, for a social order in which Jesus would feel at home. In praying this prayer, we are asking for a community into which Jesus would fit. We are asking for homes in which he could be entertained without embarrassment. We are asking for churches upon all whose ministries he could look with approval. We are asking for a city whose streets he could walk without having his heart broken. We are asking for factories and places of business into which he could go without burning with indignation. We are asking for schools that would measure up to his demands. We are asking for amusements upon which he could smile. We are asking for a literature that he could read without having his eyes blurred by tears.

Paul describes such a society when he says, "The kingdom of heaven is not eating and drinking, but righteousness and peace and joy in the Holy Spirit." To pray for the coming of the Kingdom is to pray for the coming of a reign of righteousness, justice, fair play, a chance for every human soul. It is to pray for rightness within the individual heart, rightness between man and man, rightness between capital and labor, rightness on both sides of the counter down at the store. It means, in a word, to ask that all wrong, all sin, individual and social, be dethroned, and that justice and righteousness be enthroned. It is to pray for a divine-human society where men shall live as brothers and

shall handle the tools of their daily tasks as scrupulously, as religiously as they handle their hymn books
and Bibles on Sunday morning.

Then the Kingdom of Heaven is peace. It is a peace
that is born of righteousness. If we are ever to have
real peace, it must be built upon a foundation of
righteousness. There may be a type of peace that is
born of oppression, that is the child of tyranny. But
that is not genuine peace. That is only the peace of the
graveyard. It is an ugly child of death. True peace
can live only in the heart of the individual that is right
with God and with man. And there can be no abiding
peace between man and man and nation and nation
save that which is born of righteousness and justice.
As long as we wrong and oppress one another, there
must be conflict and strife. No question is ever finally
settled until it is rightly settled. Therefore the door
into the palace of peace is righteousness.

Then the Kingdom of Heaven is joy. That is not
surprising. Joy follows upon the heels of righteousness and peace as naturally as dew sparkles at the kiss
of the sunrise. A social order builded upon justice—
a society whose every member is in possession of peace
and good will—could not fail to be a joyous society.
Many of us have found this a rather delightful world
in spite of all the injustice and strife and heartache
that so constantly war against our peace and tend to
rob us of our highest joy. What a gladsome world it
would be if every individual and every community

66

were only in the Kingdom, practicing and experiencing day by day righteousness, peace, and joy in the Holy Spirit.

Now, since the Kingdom of God means the reign of righteousness and peace and joy in every heart, and throughout the world, we are not surprised that Jesus was so enthusiastic about it. We are not surprised that he thought it of supreme worth. No wonder that he could hardly find words strong enough to express his estimate of its surpassing value. "The kingdom of heaven," he said, "is like a treasure hid in a field." To find it is like discovering unmeasured wealth. It is to experience the joyous thrill of passing from poverty to plenty, from weakness to power. It is to come into possession of a treasure infinitely more priceless than gold.

Again he said, "The kingdom of heaven is like unto a merchantman seeking goodly pearls: who, when he had found one pearl of great price, went and sold all that he had, and bought it." You can see this merchant out in quest of the best. But he finds that he has had no idea of how supremely beautiful, how wondrously worthful the best is. Then one day he makes his amazing discovery. He comes upon a pearl so surpassingly beautiful that it makes all others look like worthless gewgaws. He then gathers together all his own pearls that represent the labor of a lifetime, finds a buyer, and pushes them over the counter into his hands like so many gaudy nothings. With the money thus gained he hurries away to the owner of the priceless pearl and counts down every penny of it for the jewel that has taken captive his heart. Then having come to possess it, he takes his way home, half fearing that he must be dreaming, so great is his joy over the matchless treasure that he has in his hand.

Thus does Jesus give us his estimate of the worth of the Kingdom. Therefore, since it is of such value, it is to have first place in our hearts as it did in his own. "Seek ye first the kingdom of God, and his righteousness; and all these things shall be added unto you." We are to seek the Kingdom first, because it is first in importance. Then we are to seek it first, because it is a value that includes all lesser values. There are multitudes to-day that are in dire physical need. This is the case, not because this earth is too small or too niggardly in its gifts. It is amply able to supply every material need of every man, woman, and child. The reason it is not doing so is that we are so constantly at war with each other, either industrially or on the field of battle. We are not putting the Kingdom first. Therefore, some of us are rotting down because we have too much, others because we have too little. Failing to put first things first, we are missing the best, both materially and spiritually.

Then we are to bear in mind that when we pray, "Thy kingdom come," we are not merely asking that we may go to heaven when we die. That is surely what we shall do if we are children of the Kingdom, but that is not what we are asking here. We are praying rather that heaven may come to us while we live. This is our petition, "Thy kingdom come, thy will be done on earth as it is in heaven." In heaven God's will is perfectly obeyed. In heaven the reign of righteousness is complete. In heaven there is perfect peace. In heaven there is unmixed joy. The Kingdom is already established there. When we pray this prayer we are praying that it may be established here in our world, in our city, that we in the here and now may become a colony of heaven.

II

What is implied in this prayer?

1. When we pray "Thy kingdom come," we confess our conviction that the Kingdom has not fully come, that we live in a world that is at least partially in rebellion against God. But did not Jesus say, "The kingdom of heaven is at hand"? And did he not say, "The kingdom of God is among you"? Yes, but these sayings are in no sense contradictory to this petition. The Kingdom of God is here, now, a present fact. All round the world there are citizens of the Kingdom. But the kingship for which God is seeking is not complete. Of course there is a profound truth in the shout of the Psalmist, "The Lord reigneth!" Macbeth was reigning after a fashion when he sobbed,

"My way of life
Is fallen into the sear, the yellow leaf,
And that which should accompany old age,

69

As honor, love, obedience, troops of friends,
I must not look to have; but in their stead,
Curses not loud but deep, mouth-honor, breath,
Which the poor heart would fain deny, and dare not."

Even this bloody tyrant desired a kingship founded upon loyalty and love. Certainly a God who is our Father can be satisfied with nothing less.

But his dream is yet far from complete realization. His kingship is often but partial even in the hearts of those who confess him. I heard a preacher say the other day that all we need to settle every problem is for each man to have a good case of regeneration. And that is certainly first and fundamental. Yet something more is needed. Jesus did not only command us to disciple the nations, but to teach them as well. There was a time not so many years ago when devout Christians could hold their fellows in slavery without any compunctions of conscience. There was a time when they could engage in the liquor traffic without seeing any stains of blood upon their hands. There are still those who can live selfishly, who can be bondslaves to greed, who can be dominated by class and race prejudices, and yet fancy themselves saints. There are those who can take upon themselves the solemn vows of the Church, and live in constant forgetfulness of those vows, with never a cry of "Woe is me!" Even to those of us who claim to be his disciples, our Lord is constantly having to speak this sharp rebuke, "Why call ye me Lord, Lord, and do not the things that I say?"

Then there are vast multitudes who have never in any way acknowledged the kingship of God. The supreme tragedy of this world is the tragedy of man's rebellion against God. We are not concerned just now as to how this rebellion came about. It was not the first purpose of Jesus to explain the presence of sin in this world. But he never once shut his eyes to that grim presence. "The kingdom of heaven is likened unto a man who sowed good seed in his field; but while men slept, his enemy came and sowed tares among the wheat." And the tares are growing among the wheat till this day. When, therefore, Jesus prayed for the coming of the Kingdom, when he taught us to pray for it, he was facing the fact that the Kingdom had not fully come. Surely there is no need of an argument for the correctness of his position. Every man who is in the least thoughtful must realize that the world that now is, with its cruelties, its dark and damning sins, must be a constant heartache to our loving heavenly Father. This is certainly not the world as he means it to be. That is the reason he tells us to pray, "Thy kingdom come."

2. When we pray this prayer we not only declare our conviction that the Kingdom has not come, but we assert with equal assurance our faith that it is going to come. When Jesus turned aside from his carpenter shop that day and set out to make God King over all

men, and in every department of life, he was certainly undertaking the maddest task of which we can conceive. But he believed that it was a possible task. It was this conviction that gave him his dauntless optimism. It was this conviction that enabled him to face his own seeming failure with a quiet heart. He was absolutely sure that God was stronger than the devil. He was absolutely certain that sin in its every ghastly and hideous form should at last be driven out of the world, and that God should reign from the rivers to the ends of the earth. And when we pray we are to hold the same high expectation.

We realize, of course, that such a bracing faith is not always easy. It is exceedingly difficult in these trying times. "The far-off divine event" for which we strive seems far off indeed. No wonder that we sometimes tend to become feverish and fearful. No wonder that some ask a bit fretfully, "Where is the promise of his coming?" But remember, "It is not for you to know the times nor the seasons which the Father set in his own authority." Nor are we to worry ourselves by futile efforts at estimating the results of our ministry. Bookkeeping is not our business. It is ours to stand in our places and be true. To do this, we need courage, a courage that is born of the conviction of the absolute certainty that at last the good will win. And that conviction may be ours, for the promise is sure that one day the Kingdoms of the world shall become the Kingdoms of our Lord and his Christ.

3. When we pray this prayer we acknowledge our utter dependence upon God. If the Kingdom is ever to come, it must be through his help. All purely human schemes are doomed to failure. I believe that there is a golden age ahead of us, but the road that leads to it must be one along which he walks. Apart from him we can do nothing. "It is not by might, nor by power, but by my Spirit, saith the Lord." And it is just this Spirit that he puts at our disposal for our gigantic task. "Ye shall have power after that the Holy Spirit has come upon you." As we pray this prayer, therefore, we look for a new heaven and a new earth, wherein dwelleth righteousness. But we have no hope of attaining that goal except through him to whom all authority is given in heaven and on earth.

4. Finally, when we pray, "Thy kingdom come," we commit ourselves to the task of building the Kingdom. We recognize the fact that just as we are absolutely dependent upon God for success in this great enterprise, so is he dependent upon us. The vine can no more bear fruit without the branch than the branch without the vine. If anything is to be done toward building the Kingdom in this generation, you and I are the ones that are going to have to do it. If, therefore, we fail to put our hands to the task, then our praying is a sheer futility and little less than mockery.

Years ago our old circuit rider, who was a courageous and saintly man, preached a great sermon on "Missions." He then called upon a certain brother

73

whose "amens" had been quite ethusiastic to lead in prayer. He responded readily, and his prayer was fervent and eloquent. He prayed that the sermon might take the wings of the morning and fly to the uttermost parts of the earth. After such an earnest prayer, the preacher quite naturally thought the time fitting to take a collection to supply the wings so devoutly asked of God. But the contribution of this loud-praying brother was so shamefully small that this earnest minister had to say to him in all tenderness, "In the name of heaven, man, stop mocking God in your prayer." When we say "Thy kingdom come," we lean upon God as if all our efforts were worthless. At the same time we fling ourselves into the task as if the whole responsibility rested upon our shoulders alone.

III

Here then is a petition that is at once a prayer and a program. We are to pray it with a sense of the priceless worth of that for which we ask. We are to pray it with a realization that ours is a world in rebellion, and therefore, to that extent, a lost world. We are to pray in the firm faith that in spite of its present lostness, it is yet a solvable world. We are to pray it with a sense of our absolute dependence upon God and of his absolute dependence upon us. That we may not fail him, we are to see to it that we ourselves really enter the Kingdom. This we can do at this moment, if we have not done so already; for he says, "Him that cometh unto me, I will in no wise cast out." Then having entered, we are to live every day as children of the King, preaching, teaching, serving, conducting our daily tasks with this constantly as our goal, the building of the Kingdom of God. The whole meaning of life for us must henceforth be summed up in this one word, "Thy kingdom come."

word, "Thy kingdom come."

VI

PRAY FOR OBEDIENCE

"Thy will be done."

MATTHEW 6: 10

W E HAVE FOR OUR STUDY TO-DAY THE THIRD
petition of the Lord's Prayer—"Thy will be
done." This marks the climax of the first division of
the prayer, that division that in a peculiar sense looks
out toward God. It is easy to see how each petition
is an outgrowth and an elaboration of the one that
immediately precedes it. We pray first for the hal-
lowing of the Name. But how is God's name to be
hallowed? Only by making him King in the heart of
the individual and in the world. Therefore, we pray
"Thy kingdom come." But for what are we asking
when we pray for the coming of the Kingdom? We
are praying for a social order in which the will of God
shall be perfectly done by the group as a whole, and by
every individual in the group. In praying this prayer,
therefore, we are praying for the complete realization
of the purpose of God for the individual and for the
world. How shall we pray it?

I

We must realize something of its profound importance.

1. This petition is of vast importance, because it is the very doorway into the Kingdom. If you are a Christian, if you can say with Paul, "I know whom I have believed," there is no question as to how you won your way to that priceless knowledge. It was through the praying of this prayer with your heart, if not with your lips, "If any man is willing to do his will, he shall know." This is the doorway to the Christian life, and there is none other. God has no plan of salvation for an unsurrendered will. "Not every one that saith unto me, Lord, Lord, shall enter the kingdom; but he who doeth the will of my Father who is in heaven."

No more promising prospect came to Jesus during his entire ministry than the "Rich Young Ruler." He was a man who had kept himself without spot. When the Master tested him by the commandments, he was able to say without fear or shame, "All these have I kept from my youth." He was a man of fine courage, and with a genuine hunger for God. But when Jesus opened the door of the Kingdom to him, eager to enroll him as a subject, we read that he went away. This he did not because the Master drove him away. He failed to enter the Kingdom because he refused to pray this prayer, "Thy will be done."

But here is another who was as unpromising as the

"Young Ruler" was full of promise. He wore the livery of a foreign power. He had sold his social standing. He had sold his good name. He had sold his all in order to gain money. To the religious leaders of his time he was absolutely beyond hope. But one day he looked up from his ledger to find himself face to face with Jesus. And the Master said to him, "Follow me!" And at once this hopeless renegade rose up and followed him. And that day life for him took on a new departure. And that day he was reborn. Matthew entered the Kingdom in spite of many a handicap, because in his heart he said to Jesus, "Thy will be done." This prayer, then, is of vast importance, because there is no becoming a Christian without it.

2. Not only is this prayer the doorway into the Kingdom, but it is the whole life of the Kingdom. How strikingly this is enforced and illustrated in the life of our Lord! When we first meet him as a lad, we hear him saying, "Wist ye not that I must be about my Father's business? Do you not know that I must live my life within the will of God?" Then, after he has entered upon his ministry, we see him again at the wedding in Cana. His mother says, "They have no wine." The answer of Jesus seems almost rude: "Woman, what have I to do with thee? Mine hour has not yet come." Thus he indicates that the index finger that points to the hour at which he is to work is that of no human hand, but of his Father. Then, another day he is sitting on the curb of Jacob's well. A woman is

78

hurrying away in the distance, with a marvelous story to tell. The disciples announced dinner. But Jesus does not come. "Master, eat," they urge. But he answers, "I have meat to eat that ye know not of. My meat is to do the will of him that sent me, and to finish his work." "That is," says Jesus, "that upon which I live, that which is the source of my strength and of my power day by day, is the will of God."

At last we see him at the end of the journey. His foot is on the doorsill of the house of death. Then, as a mountain-climber might look back over the journey along which he has come, he takes a backward glance at his own life. And as he does so, he says, "I have finished the work which thou gavest me to do." By this he does not mean to say merely that he has reached the end of life. Anybody can do that. He means that his is a perfect life. As he looks back, he sees no wound left unhealed that he might have healed, no burden left unlifted that he might have lifted. His is the one perfect life, because he has lived it wholly within the will of God.

And this is what life is to mean for you and me. Out on the Damascus road one day, Paul came face to face with the risen Christ. But it was not this vision that saved him. He might have gone from that great brightness into the deepest darkness. It was his response to that vision. He said, "Lord, what wilt thou have me do?" But this one act of surrender was not enough. Paul died to self that day. But that which made him the great saint he became was that he died to self every day. Every day he reaffirmed the vow of surrender that he made when he first met his Lord. And every day we must reaffirm our vow. Every day we must be able to look up from our task and say, "To this end was I born, and for this cause came I into the world."

Then, this prayer is not only discipleship in its beginning and in its course, but also in its consummation. To surrender to God is the least we can do and be Christians at all. It is the most that we can do, both in time and in eternity. Absolutely nothing will take the place of personal surrender. Saul believed that he could make a large freewill offering a substitute for the doing of the will of God. But the voice of the Prophet was very stern and emphatic, "Behold, to obey is better than sacrifice, and to hearken than the fat of rams. Hath the Lord as great delight in burnt offerings and sacrifices, as in obeying the voice of the Lord?" However great our gifts may appear in our own eyes and in the eyes of the world, we miss the mark if we fail to live within the will of God.

On the other hand, to live within that will is perfection, however seemingly small our achievements may be. While I was a pastor in Washington, a friend told me this story: He said that a young officer just returned from France was walking down the street in the company of a young lady. This officer had gold chevrons on his sleeve in token of the fact that he had served abroad. They happened to meet a brother-officer who wore silver chevrons. The young lady asked her companion the significance of the silver, and he answered ungenerously that his brother-officer wore the silver chevrons in token of the fact that he had shown the white feather. I am told that Captain Silver proceeded to slap his face. Of course this is not the best way to settle a dispute. Yet we cannot greatly blame the captain. What is the business of a soldier anyway? Not to go to France, nor to a certain situation there. His one business is to obey orders. The man who does that rates a perfect soldier. And your job and mine is to do the will of God. Whoever does that rates as a perfect Christian.

To will aright, therefore, sums up the whole meaning of discipleship. It is Christianity in its beginning, in its course, and in its climax. Kant was right when he said that there is nothing wrong in the world but wrong will, and nothing right but right will. To will aright is to will what God wills. Christianity is, therefore, not a thing of the emotions. It is a thing of the will. Of course the emotions are vastly important, but they are important only as they set the will in motion. Emotions that do not eventuate in actions are killing things. To weep over a friend's need, and then deliberately do nothing to relieve that need, is suicidal. The whole meaning of Christianity, therefore, for time and for eternity is summed up in this prayer, "Thy will be done."

II

Then, we are to pray this prayer with the conviction that we have not fully done the will of God. This is true of us individually. How much there is of ugliness in your life and mine that would be utterly impossible if we had not so often resisted and rejected the will of God! How much of beauty and of strength and of joy would be there if we had only lived all our yesterdays within that perfect will. "Jesus beheld the city and wept over it, saying, 'I would . . . but ye would not.'" He had dreamed such a marvelous dream for this city that he loved. But its leaders refused to enter into his purpose, resisted his will, and thus lay seemingly greedy hands upon their own ruin. And that is our tragedy—God is constantly willing something for us that is so marvelously worthwhile, while we are so constantly rejecting it to choose the all-but-worthless. As we pray this prayer, therefore, we are to pray it with the consciousness that we have all sinned and come short of the glory of God.

Then, we are to pray it with the realization that what is true of us as individuals is true of the race. The tragedy of our world today is just this: There is so much being done in it every hour that is contrary to the will of God. Never forget that wherever there is social wrong, wherever there is hate, wherever one man wounds another, there the will of God is not being done. You yourself may be smarting under some tragic wrong at this moment. Maybe the one who injured you was a member of the Church. He may have even been your pastor. What then? Do not be so foolish as to blame God for that which was contrary to his will, and for which he suffers far more deeply than you.

To fail to distinguish between the good and perfect will of God and the often evil and imperfect will of man is to make shipwreck of our faith. If I had to believe that everything that is going on in this world is according to the will of God, then I could not believe in God at all. It was by making this distinction between God's will and man's will that Joseph found a firm footing upon which to stand. In his youth he had suffered a terrible injustice. He was sold into slavery out of sheer malice. But he never blamed God for the deeds of his evil brothers. "Ye meant it unto me for evil, but God meant it unto good." And because he trusted God enough to live completely within his will, God was able to change even his losses into gains, and his crosses into crowns. And so he ever does for those who thus trust him. "We know that all things work together for good to them that love God." We are to pray "Thy will be done," therefore, with the realization that much that is taking place in our own lives and in the lives of others is contrary to the will of God.

III

Then, we are to pray this prayer with earnest desire. We are to yearn above all else that the will of God may be done. We are to long for God to have his way with ourselves, with our loved ones, with our friends, with our church, with our world. Now really to desire the will of God is not always easy. Jesus himself did not find it so. At one time he faced the will of God for himself with all the natural shrinking of a man of fine and sensitive soul. As he looked toward the cross with its desertion, with its shame, with its bitter physical and spiritual agony, he was filled with a terrible dread. "Father," he prayed, "if it be possible, if there is any other way, let this cup pass from me." But always he came back to this, "Nevertheless not my will, but thine, be done."

Why did he choose the will of God in spite of the fact that it meant suffering? He chose it because he knew that the will of God was the will of his Father. He knew that the will of God was the will of one who loves with an infinite love, and who, therefore, always seeks our highest good. Not only does he seek our highest good, but he knows what that good is. We who are parents desire the highest good for our children. But so often we fail rightly to judge what is good. We blunder miserably, and the good we seek turns to be deadly evil. But God never blunders. His will is always our highest possible good. It is a perfect will.

This does not mean, of course, that in choosing the best for us, he always chooses the easiest. The will of God is a disturbing element. It is both a restraining and a constraining power. There are those who are held back, who long for a place out in the great world. Then, there are those who are thrust out who would fain remain hidden and obscure. A certain deephearted poet of the Old Testament describes God's dealings with those who live within his will under the figure of the mother eagle training her young. There is the nest 'way up among the cliffs. The young eagles are quite contented in their crude home. But one day the mother comes and ruthlessly tears the nest to pieces and flings her young out as if to let them fall to death upon the jagged rocks below. But she does not allow them to fall. She spreads abroad her wings and takes them upon her own great pinions. What is she doing? She is teaching them to fly. She is teaching them to do what they were intended to do—"to bathe their plumage in the thunder's home." And that is what God does for us who live within his will. Through all his providences, even those that seem meant to work our ruin, he is teaching us flight sunward and Godward. "I beseech you, therefore, brethren, by the mercies of God, that ye present your bodies a living sacrifice, holy, acceptable unto God, which is your reasonable service . . . that ye may prove what is that good, and acceptable, and perfect, will of God."

IV

Finally, we must pray this prayer in a spirit of self-dedication. When I say, "Thy will be done," unless I

85

am trifling, unless I am playing the hypocrite, I mean that I am here and now giving myself into his control. When I arise from my knees I am to go at once actually to doing the will of God. For, mark you, the will of God is not a passive something. We are not merely to suffer the will of God; we are to do it. "Thy will be done" is a call to battle. It is a pledging of ourselves to an aggressive campaign for the putting down of every wrong, and for the complete triumph of the right.

Now if we really commit ourselves to the doing of the will of God, we must be convinced that that will is possible. So often this is not the case. There are vast numbers, even in the Church, who have an unspoken conviction that God is asking of them more than they can do. We may never have been so bold as to put it into words, but we are in hearty agreement with the man of one talent. He said to his master frankly and to his face, "Your demands are unreasonable, you are a hard man. You reap where you do not sow. You ask of me what it is impossible for me to give." But if there was ever a slander against God, this is a slander. To do the will of God is not only possible for every one of us, but it is the one big thing that is possible. There are a thousand fine tasks that loom large in the eyes of men that you and I can never accomplish. There is no use for any of us to say, "I can do whatever another can do." I have heard the preaching of some of my brethren, and realized that such preaching

86

is forever beyond my reach. Few of us can ever be great artists. We can never be great musicians. We can never be great statesmen. We can never be men of great wealth. But we can do something better and bigger than any of these—we can do the will of God.

This is the case, not because the will of God is easy. It is utterly impossible if we go about it in our own strength. But if we will what he wills, then the impossible becomes possible. One day Jesus came face to face with a man who for more than half a lifetime had lain on the side line, a bit of human wreckage. He said to him, "Wilt thou be made whole?" In asking this question he brought home to his heart the conviction that he was willing to make him whole. But the poor fellow felt that there was no hope. But while he was telling how impossible it was, Jesus said to him, "Rise, take up thy bed, and walk." And when he willed for himself what Jesus willed for him, the power of the Infinite came into him, and the impossible became possible. And so it will be for ourselves. Give yourself to God to-day, and his own power will flow into your life. "For we are his witnesses of these things; and so is also the Holy Spirit, whom God hath given to them that obey him."

VII

PRAY FOR BREAD

"Give us this day our daily bread."
MATTHEW 6: 11

❧

I

THE FIRST AND MOST OBVIOUS LESSON THAT THIS
petition teaches is the privilege and duty of the
children of God to pray for temporal blessings. There
are those who believe in the efficacy of prayer in the
realm of the spiritual, but deny its efficacy in the realm
of what we are accustomed to call the physical. We
are to pray for grace and guidance, but we are not to
pray for rain, for instance, which is another name for
daily bread. Those holding this conviction tell us
that this is a law-abiding universe, and that to ask God
for temporal blessings is to ask that he interfere in the
operation of his own laws. Yet we realize that every
day scientists use their imperfect knowledge of these
laws in order to work results beneficent to mankind.
Surely, therefore, it is not too much to ask a fatherly
God to use his infinite knowledge of these same laws
to work results helpful to his children!

That God does answer prayer for temporal blessings is certainly taught by the Scriptures. To this, also, some of the greatest of the saints bear witness. Take George Müller, for example. He maintained his great orphanages for long years with never an appeal to anybody but God. Such a faith seems to me altogether reasonable. Since God is our Father, he is interested in all that interests us. We who are fathers and mothers can readily appreciate this. We are concerned with all the concerns of our children. We are interested in their work and their play. We are interested in their laughter and their tears. We are interested in their daily bread. There is not even a broken toy for which they care that does not concern us, however worthless that toy may be in itself. And if we being evil are thus interested in that which concerns our children, surely God is not indifferent to anything that concerns his children.

Now since God is interested in all that concerns us, he delights to have us bring these interests to himself, whether they are spiritual or material. This does not mean, of course, that he pledges himself to grant every request that we make with regard to these matters. There are two kinds of petitions that we offer. One is where the will of God is known. This is the case when we pray for what is definitely promised. When we ask, for example, for the salvation of our fellows, we can offer such a prayer without any qualification. We are explicitly told that God is not willing that any shall perish. But there are other requests that we make where we do not know the will of God. All such petitions we are to present with this qualification: "Not my will, but thine, be done."

Take the matter of praying for the sick, for instance: I am sure that God sometimes heals the sick in answer to prayer. But I am equally sure that he does not always do so. God has a plan for us in the hereafter just as surely as in the here and now. It is, therefore, not his will that every sick body should be healed. Were that the case nobody need ever die. Yet "it is appointed unto man once to die." We need to bear this in mind when we pray for the sick, or we are likely to become greatly confused.

A few years ago I knew two most excellent women to set themselves to pray for the recovery of a brother who was afflicted with tuberculosis. Such a course was altogether reasonable and right. But they presented their request without any qualification whatsoever. They prayed, so far as we could judge, without any reference to the will of God. At last they even succeeded in persuading themselves that God had granted their request. But in spite of their prayers their brother died, and their faith all but died with him. I have in mind another woman who prayed after the same fashion for her son, and when that boy passed, her whole world collapsed. And if I were going out this morning to seek for the most embittered soul that I know, I would knock at her door. She is full of rebellion against God, convinced that he broke a promise with her that, in reality, he never made. We are therefore to bring to God all our needs, but in so doing we are not to seek to bend his will to ours, but always to conform our wills to his.

Now one of our constant concerns is daily bread. Therefore we are to pray for it with full assurance that our Father is interested in what is so vital to us. I know that it is true that man shall not live by bread alone. But it is equally true that he cannot live in this present world without it. If we are souls, these souls must live in physical bodies. If we are sons of God, we are also sons of Adam. We are mixtures of deity and dust, and therefore must have bread. Of course it is very easy to overemphasize the bread question. That we have done. But the cure for that evil is not found by ignoring bread altogether. The God who is not willing that any shall perish for lack of spiritual bread is also unwilling that any shall perish for lack of material bread. There is nobody starving in our world of plenty this morning who is doing so in accordance with the will of God.

Jesus indicated his keen concern for our physical needs when he lived among us. The first miracle that he wrought was to supply wine for the guests at an obscure wedding feast to which he and a few friends had been invited. Then, more than once he fed the hungry multitudes that waited upon his ministry. On one occasion we see him teaching and healing through the long day till the shadows lengthen. The disciples become restless. At last they break in upon the Master with this suggestion: "Send the multitudes away, that they may go into the villages, and buy themselves food." But Jesus answers, "They need not depart; give ye them to eat." Their hunger was a cry to him for daily bread, a cry to which he responded by amply meeting their needs.

And as he was on this side of the cross, so we find him after his resurrection. Here is one of the most beautiful stories in the Gospels. Simon Peter, with a few of his friends, has gone back to his old task of fishing. Through the long night they have toiled, and have taken nothing. And now they are coming home empty-handed. I can appreciate their position. Most of the good catches that I have known took place the day before I got there, or the day after I left. As they come to the shore over the dawn-lit sea, they find the Master waiting for them. "Come and break your fast," he says. How perfectly winsome! "All things were made by him, and without him was not anything made that was made." Yet he is not above preparing breakfast for a little handful of fishermen who have come in from a fruitless night of toil. It is to a God like this that we pray, "Give us this day our daily bread."

II

Then this prayer indicates our complete dependence upon God for our daily bread. It is rather strange that we recognize our dependence upon him for the Bread of Life so much more readily than we do for our physical bread. All who are believers are ready to confess our inability to save ourselves spiritually. We quote with approval the words of St. Paul, "By grace are ye saved through faith, and that not of yourselves: it is the gift of God." We recognize the fact that while the devil pays wages, God never does. "The wages of sin is death; but the gift of God is eternal life through Jesus Christ our Lord." "Repent," we quote again, "and be baptized every one of you in the name of Jesus, . . . and ye shall receive the gift of the Holy Spirit." We do not earn eternal life. We receive it as a gift.

But the Bread of Life is no more a gift from God than is the material bread upon which we nourish our bodies day by day. "Every good and every perfect gift is from above." Our Father in heaven is not a merchant that sells; he is a King that gives. Every blessing must come from his loving hand. Apart from him, the wisest of us could no more create a loaf of ordinary bread than we could create a universe. All food comes from the earth, and "the earth is the Lord's, and the fullness thereof." He must send the sunshine and the rain in order for the earth to "give seed to the sower and bread to the eater." Should God cease to give, every vestige of life would vanish from our world. We are just as dependent upon him,

93

therefore, for our daily bread as for the gift of the Holy Spirit.

For this reason all need to pray this prayer. It is a prayer for the poor. It is a prayer for the father whose pockets are empty. It is a prayer for the mother at whose skirts hungry children are plucking and asking for bread that she cannot give. But it is a prayer no less for the rich. It is as truly for the multimillionaire as it is for the beggar. For what is the wealth of the money-magnate worth to him if God withholds the gift of bread? He cannot live on silver and gold and stocks and bonds. You remember the old story of how Midas longed above all else to have the power of turning everything that he touched into gold? When that power was granted, he went about his palace touching this and that, and feeling that his wealth was piling up by the millions. But when he grew hungry, his bread turned to gold, and the water became gold at the touch of his thirsty lips. And he found that all his wealth was only dust and ashes if God fails to give bread.

All, then, are equally dependent upon God. The only difference between the rich and the poor in this matter is that wealth tends to blind us to our dependence. That is one of its greatest dangers. We have never taken Jesus quite seriously when he says, "How hard it is for them that have riches to enter the kingdom." Yet even he never said a truer word. And one thing that makes riches so dangerous is that they

94

often give their possessor a sense of independence toward God. That is what they did for the Rich Farmer. That is the reason that Jesus called him a fool. Every man is a fool who thinks himself independent of God, whether he lives in a palace or on a bench in the park. We are to pray this prayer, therefore, all of us, with a sense of our complete dependence on God.

III

Then, this is an unselfish prayer. It is a prayer that requires a brotherly heart of him who prays it. We are not encouraged to say, "Give me this day my daily bread." We are to pray for others as well as for ourselves. This is the prayer of one who loves his neighbors as he loves himself. To pray this prayer as Jesus longs that it be prayed would result in blessings beautiful almost beyond our dreams. It would mean that a world where there is much of want would be a world of plenty. It would mean a world of coöperation instead of a world of competition. It would mean literally a new earth wherein dwelleth righteousness.

If I am an employer, to pray this prayer means that I am going to give a just wage to my brother who works for me. To say "Give us our daily bread," and then do my best to wrench his out of his hand is sheerest mockery. Jesus knew certain Pharisees who robbed widows' houses, and to cover up their rascality prayed long prayers. Possibly they even asked God to supply the need of those widows that they themselves had impoverished. But there was no worth in their prayers. They only received to themselves the greater damnation. The same law holds for me as for an employee. If I pray this prayer, I am to give to my employer a just and honest day's work for the wages received. To fail to do so is to play the hypocrite.

The plain truth is that this prayer is possible only for those who are willing to do the right as God gives them to see the right. We cannot ask him for bread that has upon it any taint of fraud or injustice. Our nation is now making a heroic effort at economic recovery. We cannot look on without admiration. But with our admiration there is also deep concern. We read only yesterday where one was boasting proudly of the fact that our government was soon to be getting $500,000,000 a year in revenue from the sale of liquor. But how can we as a Christian nation honestly pray for bread that comes from that source? Such bread is poisoned by the blighted manhood and womanhood that go into its making. It is wet with the tears of despoiled and handicapped childhood. The bread that God gives is clean bread, and we can honestly pray for no other kind.

Then to pray this prayer means that we shall be willing to share with our brothers. "There was a certain rich man, which was clothed in purple and fine linen, and fared sumptuously every day: and there was a certain beggar named Lazarus, which was laid at his gate, full of sores, and desiring to be fed with the crumbs which fell from the rich man's table." This rich man, being religious, prayed, "Give us this day our daily bread." And God answered by giving him more than enough. He made him a trustee for his sick brother that lay at his gate. But the rich man betrayed his trust. He held himself aloof and flung him only the crumbs. Thus he became separated from him by a chasm that grew wider and wider till it became as wide as that which separates heaven from hell. And such chasms will always exist in a world where men pray this prayer with their lips, and then fail to play a brother's part when they rise from their knees.

IV

Notice, finally, the reasonableness of this prayer.

1. It is reasonable because in praying it we ask only for what we need. When we pray for daily bread, we are not asking for a fortune. We are not asking God to let us corner the food market. We are not asking for a palace on the Avenue. We are not asking for high social position. We are not asking for ropes of pearls, nor for high-powered cars. We are asking for what God promises, and for that only. "My God shall supply," not all your whims, not all your desires, but "all your needs, according to his riches in glory by Christ Jesus." As a rule he gives us far beyond our needs. But it is only for the supply of our actual needs that we are told to pray.

2. In praying this prayer we are asking for bread

that is justly ours. I think Dr. Dods is right in giving this interpretation. We are asking for bread that we have coöperated with God in winning. Every promise of our heavenly Father is conditional. We do not expect the gift of salvation except at the price of our personal surrender. And just as we must coöperate with God in order to receive the spiritual blessings that he delights to give, so must we coöperate with him in order to receive our daily bread. My father as a devout Christian farmer was accustomed to pray this prayer. But he always prayed it with the conviction that he must coöperate with God, if he was to receive the desired blessing. To fail to do so is not faith, but presumption. Suppose, for instance, he had prayed this prayer, telling God to plant corn in one field and to sow wheat in another, while he himself sat in the shade and did naked nothing. He would simply have starved and his whole family with him. When we pray for our daily bread, therefore, we pray for bread that we coöperate with God in making.

And remember that God requires this coöperation, not as a punishment, but for our highest good. The old idea was that work was sent on us as a curse. But nothing could be further from the truth. Work is a great blessing. It is a blessing without which man cannot adequately live. To get without giving is deadly. An idle man, like a vacant house, soons falls into ruins. I believe in organized charity, but it is a poor second best. Few greater calamities could come to the needy among us than to be permanently supported without work. Rome rotted down while being coddled by free shows and free feeds. This prayer, therefore, is not only asking for daily bread, but it is asking for what is of equal importance—an opportunity to earn that bread. That opportunity is not available to every man to-day. This is the case, not because God has failed us, but because we have failed him. We have so grossly misused the world that he has committed to our charge that millions are being robbed of a chance to work. We are seeking a cure for this evil when we pray this prayer.

As we face these facts we are able to realize something of the vast wealth and worth of this petition. It gives us a guarantee of our right to bring every temporal need of our lives before God. It looks toward the making of a new social order where I shall be partner to every man, and every man shall be partner to me, and all shall be partners with God. It means the consecration of our daily tasks. And as in the long ago Jesus was known in the breaking of bread, so, as we rightly pray this prayer, he is known to us. It enables us to see upon every loaf that comes to our tables the finger marks of God, and to make of every meal a sacrament. Therefore, may the Lord help us to pray with sincere hearts, "Give us this day our daily bread."

PRAY FOR BREAD

VIII

PRAY FOR FORGIVENESS

"Forgive us our trespasses, as we forgive those who trespass against us."

MATTHEW 6: 12

I

THIS PRAYER FOR FORGIVENESS MEETS A DEMAND that is just as universal as is that for daily bread. All of us need to pray it, because we have all sinned. I am quite aware that sensitiveness toward sin is by no means an outstanding characteristic of our generation. Our consciences seem to have become strangely benumbed. There are multitudes of us who fancy that we have run clean past all need of this petition. We never think of praying it at all. There are others who pray it after a fashion, but with a distressing lack of reality and earnestness. It is an easy utterance of our lips rather than an anguished cry of our hearts that is red with shame and wet with tears.

But the fact that we are not worried over our sins does not by any means prove our innocence. Our lack of pain is no positive indication of our spiritual health.

I was at the bedside of a boy some time ago who was dying of a certain type of cancer. His face had swollen till one eye had burst from its socket. But I was told that he was not suffering the slightest pain. But the fact that there was no pain was not a guarantee either of present or returning health. It meant only that the disease had killed the sensory nerves. Therefore, in spite of the absence of all pain, death was creeping upon him with sure and stealthy feet. Even so our lack of sensitiveness to sin is not a proof of our spiritual health, but rather of the opposite.

The whole Bible is written on the assumption that man is a sinner. It declares emphatically that "all have sinned and come short of the glory of God." And in so saying, it speaks home to the deepest consciousness of the race. We may compare ourselves among ourselves with little sense of guilt. We may shut our eyes at times to our own moral ugliness. We may stop our ears in some measure to the outcries of conscience. We may administer sedatives to our souls with this and that excuse. But with all this, there is not a man of us who, when he dares honestly face the facts about himself, can deny in good conscience that he is a sinner. This Book, broadly speaking, gives two distinct definitions of sin. At the bar of both of these, all of us must needs plead guilty.

First, sin is the transgression of the law. Sin is doing what we know to be wrong. It is the choice of the lower rather than of the higher. It is doing the thing that we know we ought not to do. It is thinking the thoughts that we know we ought not to think. It is taking the pleasure that we know we ought not to take. It is inflicting the wound that we know we ought not to inflict. It is speaking the word that we know we have no right to speak. Sin is wrongdoing, and who in all the world can honestly say that he has never been guilty of a single wrong?

Then, the Bible defines sin as failure in right-doing. "To him that knoweth to do good, and doeth it not, to him it is sin." It is vastly arresting, as we have noted before, that Jesus introduces a new type of villain. The villain of the ordinary type is one who does some aggressive wrong. He is the perpetrator of positive evil. But such is not the case with the villain of Jesus. He is passive rather than active. For instance, he told of a certain fig tree that was to be cut down, not because it bore poisonous fruit, but because it bore no fruit at all. The man of one talent was flung out into the night, not because he had squandered his lord's money, but because he had failed to make a right use of it. The Priest and the Levite had to take their places in the prisoner's dock, along with certain brigands, not because they had plotted a crime or had shared its reward, but because they had passed a wounded man that others had robbed, and had left him unhelped. Dives lifted up his eyes in hell, not because he had killed the beggar that lay at his gate by thrusting him through his heart, but because he had killed him by letting him alone.

Sin, then, is wrongdoing. It is also failure in right-doing. And who of us has always been in when duty came and knocked at his door? Who has rendered every service that was within his power to render? Who has lifted every load that he might have lifted? Who has given all that he might have given? Not one of us. The book of your life-story and mine is kept open by blighted flowers of opportunity. We have lived to some purposes, thank God! But the contribution we have made is only a meager fraction of what it might have been. We have not done our best. We have all sinned and come short.

Then, we have not only failed in right-doing, but in right-being. How far we are from the realization of Christ's great dream for us! "What do ye more than others?" he asks of us this morning as he asked of his disciples in the long ago. He means that his presence shall make such a vast difference in our lives. But in spite of all that he offers, we somehow remain quite ordinary and commonplace. The tragedy of Samson's broken vow was not that he became worse than other men, but rather that he became like other men, when God had called him to be vastly different. What pigmies we are in comparison with the men and women that God made it possible for us to be! How wanting in spiritual duty, when God is longing that we shall have something of the beauty and winsomeness of

103

Jesus! We have failed, every one of us, to measure up to our highest possibilities.

And just as we have failed as individuals, we have failed as a Church. What a compelling and irresistible something was the youthful Church just after Pentecost! Small in numbers, destitute of wealth, and of social position, it yet swept over the world with irresistible power, making the wilderness and the solitary place to become glad, and the desert to rejoice and to blossom as a rose. We have strong and rich and influential churches to-day. But there are all too few powerful churches. The promise is, "Ye shall receive power, after that the Holy Spirit is come upon you." We are to be mighty with the very might of God. But too often this is not the case. In the midst of one of the most needy generations that the world has ever seen, we are pitifully impotent. For our perplexed and bewildered day, too few of us have any sure word from God. Neither as individuals nor as a church have we possessed our possessions. Therefore, we all need to pray for forgiveness.

Then, we all need to pray for forgiveness, because God alone can forgive. We cannot wash the stains from our own hands any more than could Lady Macbeth. We cannot earn this forgiveness. It must come to us as a gift of God. And the Bible seems to have been written for this one purpose—to tell us of God's infinite eagerness and ability to forgive. As we turn the pages of the Old Testament, one radiant-faced saint after another bears witness to the forgiving grace of God. "Who is a God likened to our God; that pardoneth iniquity?" we hear one sing, "He will cast all our sins into the depths of the sea." "As far as the east is from the west, so far has he removed our transgressions from us," shouts another. "And what he has done for us," they declare, "he will do for you." "Let the wicked forsake his way, and the unrighteous man his thoughts: and let him return unto the Lord, and he will have mercy upon him: and to our God, for he will abundantly pardon."

And when we come to the New Testament, we find the same great story only with a clearer certainty, and a greater note of joy. Here we come face to face with One who declares that he has not come to call the righteous, but sinners to repentence. He is out to seek and to save that which is lost. He tells of a certain graceless laddie who wasted his substance with harlots. But when, broken in heart and hope, he came home, his father did not give a place in the servants' quarters as the son asked him to do. Instead, he gave him a kiss of welcome, put a ring on his hand and shoes on his feet. He gave him himself, with all the love of his big, tender heart. "And that," said Jesus, "God will do for every one that will ask him."

II

But what do we mean by forgiveness? There are those who think of forgiveness as a rather trifling matter. Some think of it, for instance, as no more than an escape from punishment. It is the remission of a penalty. But forgiveness must go far deeper than that. You remember how Beauty Steele in the *Right of Way* pleaded the cause of a client of his who was accused of murder. Through his impassioned appeal the jury brought in a verdict of "Not Guilty." The accused man upon whom the shadow of the gallows had been falling was allowed to go free. In his gratitude, he hurried to the lawyer, in order to thank him. But the man that had saved his life drew away in disgust, saying, "Off with you; you are as guilty as hell." This man went free, but he was not forgiven.

Then, forgiveness is something more than a way of escape from the consequences of our sin. There are times when forgiveness does save us from some of the consequences of wrongdoing. Harold Bigbie gives us an instance of this in his story of "Old Born Drunk." This man had been made drunk in his very infancy. He had literally soaked in liquor for more than half a lifetime. But under the ministry of the Angel Adjutant he was converted. His sins were forgiven. And from that hour all desire for drink was taken away. But this is not always the case. In truth it is the exception rather than the rule. I have in mind another drunkard who was converted just as genuinely as "Old Born Drunk." But I shall never forget having that man tell me that there had not been an hour since his conversion that he wouldn't have give his right arm for one drink of liquor.

What, then, is forgiveness? What, for instance, does it mean for one man to forgive another? Here are two who have once been friends. But love has changed to hate, and hate has led to separation. They no longer have any fellowship with each other. They pass each other on the street without speaking. But something happens to bring them together. They forgive and receive forgiveness. And what is the result? They love and trust each other as in the old days. And so it is when God forgives. The estrangement that sin has wrought is done away, and God trusts us, and we trust God. Forgiveness, therefore, means reconciliation. Because it means this, it has its issue in a new man. The Governor may pardon a thief, but he will be a thief still. But when God pardons a thief, he makes him into an honest man. To be forgiven, therefore, is to be a new creation in Christ Jesus.

III

How is this forgiveness to become ours?

This prayer teaches that it may be ours for the asking. But in thus asking for forgiveness, we, of course, pledge ourselves to give up all known sin. Now, the one sin that is specifically mentioned is the sin of hate. "If you forgive men their trespasses, your Father who is in heaven will also forgive you your trespasses." But there is no forgiveness possible on any other grounds. There may be some one against whom you are nursing a grudge. That some one may have wronged you genuinely and deeply. It may have been a wrong for which you feel that there is no possible remedy. But however genuine your grievance, however hardened and impenitent the wrongdoer, and however long he may have persisted in his offenses, you must forgive, not once, but until seventy times seven. This you must do, or there is no possible forgiveness for you.

This is the case, not because Christ is unwilling to forgive the unforgiving, but because it is impossible for him to do so. "When ye stand praying, forgive, if ye have aught against any: that your Father also who is in heaven may forgive you." God is eager to forgive all of us, even the unforgiving. But till we are willing to forgive, he simply cannot forgive us. This is the case because of what forgiveness involves. To be forgiven is to be a new creation. It is to have peace with God, and peace with our fellows. It is to have hate changed into love. "We know that we have passed out of death into life, because we love." But to ask God to make you a new creation, while you keep your old hating heart, is to ask for a rank impossibility. God can no more forgive the unforgiving than he can make our world radiant with morning and black with night at the same time.

The truth of the matter is that you cannot really pray this prayer unless you are willing to forgive. You are not saying to God, "Forgive me my trespasses." You are saying, "Forgive us"—that is, "Forgive me, and forgive the man that I hate—forgive the man on whom I desire to inflict pain. Forgive the man that I do not forgive myself." But the fact that you do not forgive him means that you do not desire him to be forgiven. Thus you are asking God for what you do not desire at all. Then we are to ask for forgiveness in proportion to that we give. If, therefore, we fail to forgive, we are praying, "Lord, I am going to get even with this man if it takes me a lifetime. Do thou in thy might and wisdom and power get even with me." Here, then, is a law that is as fixed as the law of gravitation. In order to receive forgiveness we must be willing to forgive.

IV

Perhaps there are those who feel that genuine forgiveness on their part is impossible. In order to help you, I offer these two suggestions:

1. Remember that in allowing yourself to hate you are doing yourself the greatest possible injury. Your unforgiving spirit is a grief to God. It may lead you to do harm to the object of your dislike. But one thing is absolutely certain; it is working and will continue to work untold injury to yourself. Hate and hell always live in the same heart. This is true in the here and now. It will be true forever. Of all the sins that eat like acid into the soul, there is none equal to this. I

have known some miserable people in my life. But if I were in search of the most miserable man in the world this morning, I would know exactly where to find him. I would knock on the door of the best hater in the world. Therefore, if you would know a moment's joy, avoid hate as you would avoid the flames of hell.

2. But our greatest help toward a forgiving heart is the remembrance of God's forgiveness to us. Jesus told a story of a certain king that set about the task of reckoning with his servants. A poor fellow was brought before him who had become hopelessly involved. He owed millions, and he had not a penny with which to pay. His king, not willing to lose the whole debt, ordered the man to be sold into slavery, and his wife and children as well. What a tragic plight! No wonder the poor fellow, when he realized that his debt meant ruin, not only to himself, but to those whom he loved, fell upon his face and pleaded for time, "Have patience with me," he begged, "and I will pay thee all." And the king out of pure kindness of heart did far more. He canceled his entire debt, and sent him away a free man. When I met him a little later I could hardly recognize him. His eyes sparkled, his face looked as if it had a sunrise behind it. His stooped shoulders were squared. He seemed like a new man.

"What in the world has happened?" I asked in amazement. "Why, the most wonderful thing imag-

inable," he answered. "An hour ago I was hopeless,
without a penny between me and slavery, both of myself and of my wife and children. It seemed more
than I could bear. In utter desperation I begged for a
little time to settle my enormous debt. But His Majesty did far more. He canceled the debt altogether."
But a moment later I glanced at my friend, to discover
that the light had gone out of his eyes. His face had
become hard, and sunless, and sinister. While I was
wondering what had caused this terrible change, he
suddenly seized a shabbily-dressed man by the collar,
and snarled at him, "Pay me that $15 you owe me."
And this poor fellow flung himself down and prayed
the same prayer that his harsh creditor had prayed just
a few moments ago. But his plea was in vain. The
face that bent above him did not soften. Instead, it
became only the more hard and cruel, with the result
that he had the pitiful bankrupt cast into prison. That
was tragic enough, but infinitely more tragic was the
fate of the unforgiven man himself.

And what was the result for the man whose heart
was not softened toward his brother by the mercy that
had been shown to himself? The answer is obvious
and inevitable. His king canceled his forgiveness, and
had him cast into prison. It could not have been otherwise. The unforgiving man himself had already canceled that forgiveness by refusing to forgive. He had
already cast himself into a dungeon darker than any
built by human hands by harboring hate in his heart.

"And so likewise," said Jesus, "shall my heavenly Father do also unto you, if ye from your hearts forgive not every one his brother their trespasses." We must forgive, because hate is hell. We must forgive because One whom we have crucified and put to open shame is even now offering us forgiveness. It is, therefore, in the realization of the deadliness of hate, and in the realization of the goodness of God in forgiving us infinitely more than we can ever be called upon to forgive, that we are to pray this prayer—"Forgive us our trespasses, as we forgive those who trespass against us."

IX

PRAY AGAINST TEMPTATION
"Lead us not into temptation."
MATTHEW 6: 13

I

ALL OF US KNOW SOMETHING OF TEMPTATION. We have had more or less to do with it from our youth. It is a part of the personal experience of every one of us. In our study of this petition, therefore, we find ourselves on familiar ground. What is temptation? As used in the Scriptures, the word has two common meanings.

1. Temptation is an inducement to evil. It is an appealing invitation to take the wrong road. It is this type of temptation that is pictured for us on the first pages of the Book of Genesis. "Has God said that you are not to eat of every tree of the garden?" the serpent is represented as asking Eve. "We may eat of every tree except one," the woman answers. "The only one that is forbidden is the tree of the knowledge of good and of evil. If we eat of that, we shall surely die." "You shall not surely die," is the emphatic de-

113

nial. "On the contrary you will be as gods, knowing good and evil." Here, then, is an alluring promise of a larger life. But to win this life, it is necessary to go against the known "Thou-shall-not" of God. The voice of inclination is calling in the opposite direction to the voice of conscience. Thus Eve was tempted in the long ago, and thus we are tempted to-day.

Now, temptation may come from within or from without. "Every man is tempted," says James, "when he is drawn away of his own lust, or desire, and enticed." That is, we may be tempted when no one is making any effort to tempt us. We may look upon those who are in better circumstances than ourselves and become envious or covetous. We may look upon those worse off than we and become contemptuous. We may become puffed with pride over our own real or fancied beauty or intellectual gifts, or we may grow bitter and sour over our lack of these gifts. There are countless occasions for temptation arising out of our own evil hearts. Then, we may be tempted through agencies or influences outside ourselves. "My son," warns a certain writer of the Old Testament, "if sinners entice thee, consent thou not." Here is an inducement to do wrong that comes from a wrong companionship. Such may teach us through heart-breaking experience the truth of that declaration: "The companion of fools shall be destroyed."

But there is one source from which temptation toward evil never comes, and that is from God. "Let

no man say when he is tempted, I am tempted of God:
for God cannot be tempted with evil, neither tempteth
he any man." "That is," says wise and practical James,
"God never invites any man to take the lower road."
It certainly ought to be easy for us to accept this. Yet
how many wrongs have been wrought by those who
claimed divine authority for their deeds! Some of the
blackest crimes of history have been committed in the
name of religion. Temptation is always dangerous,
but it is never so deadly dangerous as when we per-
suade ourselves that the voice that calls us to take the
wrong road is the voice of God.

Some years ago I was preaching a sermon that was
evidently going forward to the great satisfaction of
at least one listener. He was responding by an almost
continuous flow of hearty "Amens." At first I was
delighted. Soon, however, I became suspicious that his
enjoyment was born of his zest for hearing the denun-
ciation of the other man's sin. Finally, I said a word
about the importance of being actively identified with
some church. I even administered a sharp rebuke to
those who held aloof from the church because they
fancied themselves too good to belong. At once a deep
silence fell upon him. After the service I found that
from an earnest supporter of the Church, he had become an aggressive enemy. But he had done the right
thing in changing from a helper to a hinderer. He declared that the Lord had told him to do what he was
doing. "Come out from among them, and be ye sep-

arate," he quoted pridefully. But Jesus took no such attitude toward the Church in his day. It was at a low spiritual ebb. But he never allowed that fact to keep him away. "He went up into the synagogue on the Sabbath day, as his custom was." He never left off his habit of church attendance. Temptation, then, is an invitation to do wrong. But such an invitation never comes from God.

2. Temptation means a test or a trial. This is the meaning that it has in our text. Such tests, when met along the path of duty, are intended for our good. They are to minister to our strength and to our growth in Christlikeness. They are to do for us what the sculptor does for the rude block of marble. They are to bring to light the angel that is pent up within us. We are never called upon to meet a testing of any kind but that God is there, inviting us to take the upward way. He is always there offering us the undergirding of his everlasting arms. If we are only wise enough to hear his voice and accept his help, our victory is an absolute certainty.

But while God never leads us into temptation except for our good, such tests always have in them possibilities of disaster. When a teacher gives his class a test, his purpose is not the failure of the class, though failure is a possibility. Otherwise the test is not real. When a manufacturer turns out a new car, he tests it. His purpose is not to wreck it, though it may become a wreck in the process. Even so, the tests that you and

I have to face are God's upward calls to us; but they prove our undoing by our refusal to respond to that upward call. However, of this we may be sure, that we never stand at the forks of the road, but that God is there, wooing us to take the right turn. Temptation, therefore, as used in our text has two sides, a lower and a higher. Every test has a downward call; but always its primary purpose, assuming that we are within the will of God, is to lead us to a firmer choice of right.

II

Now, though we are commanded to pray, "Lead us not into temptation," yet into temptation God does lead us day by day. This does not mean, of course, that all the tests that we meet are of his choosing. Some are born of our own willfulness. But there are others that are a part of God's wise purpose for us. This is evidenced by the fact that to live in a world like ours is to be tempted. Temptation is a universal human experience. There is no possible escape from it. Of course we can narrow in some measure the range of our temptations, and lessen their intensity. But to escape them altogether is an impossibility.

We may help ourselves, for instance, by a wholesome environment. A survey of our city has shown that juvenile delinquency grows less the farther we get away from our slum section. There are boys and girls growing up only a few blocks from this church under circumstances that make a clean and wholesome manhood and womanhood next to impossible. When we pray this prayer, therefore, we are praying that we ourselves and all of our fellows may have the cleanest possible environment. We cannot thus pray and be indifferent to the home-life, to the amusements, to the working conditions of our fellows. We cannot thus pray, and vote for an increase of temptation through the return of the open saloon. But while a wholesome environment is a great safeguard, while it increases our chances of victory, it does not exempt us from temptation altogether.

And, just as environment is not an absolute safeguard against temptation, no more is good birth. Now it is a great privilege to be well-born. If the sins of the parents are visited upon their children to the third and fourth generations, so are their virtues. If it is possible for us to stand at the upstairs windows of life and pour red-hot acid into the faces of our children that come after us, so is it possible for us to pour into their hearts the moral momentum of a clean and pious ancestry. There are some temptations that dog the steps of one man to which another is an absolute stranger. Take the matter of drink, for instance. What a constant and terrible temptation it is to some that we know. But to others it is no more a temptation than a score of other kinds of deadly poison. This is often the case because these latter have been born of a sober ancestry. But while to be well-born is a help, it does not exempt from temptation altogether.

Then, no degree of moral and spiritual attainment can exempt us from temptation. Of course such attainment is an immense help. The more we yield to temptation, the weaker we become. But the opposite is also true: the more we triumph, the stronger we become. Yet triumph how we may, temptation persists to the end of the journey. I have met those who claimed that they had climbed so far into the spiritual heights that they were no longer tempted. But of course they were grossly self-deceived. For me to make such claim would be to declare that I had run clean past Jesus, and was looking back at him. He knew no sin, yet "he was in all points tempted like as we are." We are to pray this prayer, therefore, with the realization that temptation is a universal human experience.

All of us are tempted, because temptation is for our good. It is a part of God's wise plan for us. It was a part of his plan for Jesus. "Then was Jesus led up of the Spirit into the wilderness to be tempted of the devil." He was not tempted by mere chance. He was tempted according to the purpose of God. It is even so with ourselves. I know there are those who bewail the fact that this is the case. They join sorrowfully with Omar Khayyam in his pathetic wail:

"Oh, could we but grasp this sorry scheme of things entire,
 Would we not wreck it and mould it nearer to the heart's desire?"

These are yearning for a world where life is easy, where there are no desperate battles in which they may lose or win their souls.

But the Apostle James takes the opposite view. He faces the fact that life is a rather dangerous adventure. But instead of wailing over it, he rather rejoices. Instead of pitying us because of our hard road, he rather congratulates us. In truth, instead of sobbing over the grim fact of temptation, he grows quite enthusiastic about it. "Count it all joy," he shouts, "when you fall into divers temptations. It is God's way of growing a soul." Therefore, "blessed is the man that endureth temptation, for when he is tried, he shall receive the crown of life, which the Lord has promised to them that love him." God can grow an oyster without temptation, but not a man. Character is only achieved in a realm of choices. It is a child of conflict. Therefore, though we pray, "Lead us not into temptation," we do so, knowing that temptation is universal, and that it is the only way that God has of growing a soul.

III

If, then, there is no escape from temptation, why pray this prayer? To my mind, the answer is plain. This is the prayer of a forgiven man. We have just asked in the previous petition for the forgiveness of our sins. Having so asked, we have come into the consciousness that God has heard our prayer, and has taken us back into his fellowship. We have just come to sing:

> "My God is reconciled,
>   His pardoning voice I hear.
> He owns me for his child,
>   I can no longer fear."

Having had the tragic quarrel between ourselves and God healed, having come to enjoy the light of his countenance, how are we to face the future? How are we to keep this beautiful relationship into which God's forgiving love has brought us? Having been made anew, how are we to walk before him in newness of life? We are to do so by having this prayer within our hearts and upon our lips: "Lead us not into temptation." We are to pray thus for the following reasons:

1. Because we realize the deadly danger of sin. What Jesus said to the man whom he had healed after a sickness of thirty and eight years was this: "Sin no more, lest a worse thing come to thee." This bit of human wreckage had just been remade. He had been set upon his feet a new man. But Jesus reminds him of the foe that worked his ruin in other days. He tells him that it was sin that had forced him to lie for more than half a lifetime in impotent usefulness. He warns him further that for him to fall again will result in deeper tragedy than that from which he has just been delivered. And what he said to this man, he says to every healed soul among us, and that is, "Sin no more."

What, then, is to be the deepest dread of every for-given man? What is your deepest dread? From what do you shrink more than from all else? Life for many of us is beset by fears. Some are afraid of microbes and germs. Some are afraid of suffering. Some are afraid of poverty. Some are dreadfully afraid of dis-comfort. Some fear unpopularity and criticism. Some are afraid of death. But the one thing that we ought to fear is sin. That was the case with that little hand-ful of saints just after Pentecost. Persecution was abroad, but when they bowed the knee for prayer, for what did they ask? Not for deliverance from shame or death. "And now, Lord, behold their threatening: and grant unto thy servants, that with all boldness they may speak thy word." Their one gripping fear was that, in the face of a great opportunity, they might fall into the dire and damning sin of cowardice. And because we, too, realize that sin may undo for us all that the forgiving love of God has done, we are to pray this prayer, "Lead us not into temptation."

2. We are to pray this prayer because we realize our own weakness. We know from actual experience that in our own strength we cannot triumph over our temp-tations. Overconfidence has been responsible for count-less failures in every department of life. The other day it was my privilege to see an exciting football game. It was easy to see, as soon as the two teams marched upon the field, that one was considerably heavier than

the other. There was hardly a question in anybody's mind as to the easy victory of this heavier team. Least of all, I am confident, was there any question in the mind of that team itself. The whole organization fairly swaggered as they went into position. But the lighter team won. It owed its victory, partly to good playing, but more to the overconfidence of its opponents.

When I was a boy, my brother and I spent almost half a day catching a little, knotty, hidebound, runty yearling. We put a rope about his stubby horns, and led him up to the barn. Here we called a colored playmate of ours, and challenged him to ride the beast. This colored friend was himself almost as large as the yearling. He accepted our challenge with obvious contempt. He looked to see the little runt crash under him. Now my brother's part was to accidently turn the yearling loose at the proper time, and mine was to crank him. The result for the overconfident rider was disastrous. He could only remark as he picked himself up out of the mud, that if he had known that the yearling had so much fight in him he would have stuck a little tighter.

A certain aged minister of our Church tells this story. A good many years ago a drunkard in the town where he was pastor was converted and joined his Church. In the old days, before his conversion, he used to ride into town almost every day and hitch his horse to a certain post in front of the Corner Saloon.

After his conversion, in spite of repeated warnings from his faithful pastor, he still hitched his horse to that same hitching post. At last he fell into his old habit of drink, and according to the customs of that day was tried and expelled from the Church. What was the secret of his downfall? It was overconfidence. What he needed was to pray this prayer, and then to prove his sincerity by getting a new hitching post as far from that saloon as possible. "Let him that thinketh he standeth take heed lest he fall."

3. Then, we are to pray, "Lead us not into temptation," with the full assurance that if we give God the ordering of our lives, he will be our sufficiency, that he will make us conquerers, and more than conquerers through him that loves us. Here is a side of the gospel that receives too little emphasis in our day. The Christian life is to be a life of victory. We are not to be overcome of evil, whatever may be the nature of that evil. But we are to overcome evil with good. If the Bible teaches anything with emphasis, it is this, that God stands ready to enable us to deal mightily and victoriously with every temptation that we may be called upon to meet. "In that he has suffered, being tempted, he is able to succor them that are tempted." "God is faithful who will not suffer you to be tempted above that ye are able, but will with the temptation make a way of escape that ye may be able to bear it." "God is faithful." That is the firm conviction of the

writers of the New Testament. He may be counted upon absolutely. He will never fail us nor forsake us.

Not only will he bring us through the fiery furnace without the smell of fire upon our garments if we trust him, but he will make us vastly richer through the very experiences that seem sent only to work our ruin. I am speaking to some who, even now, are being sorely tried. Some of you have lost your wealth. Some have lost your health. Some have lost treasures infinitely more precious than these. What can I say to such perplexed and bewildered souls? I can offer this prayer as a strong staff upon which to lean. Cry to your Father, "Lead us not into temptation," and he will not fail you. He will bring you through to a victory that will be a surprise to your own hearts. He will enable you to say with another who had suffered wounds more grievous than you, "We know that all things"—the glad things and the sad things; the things that make our eyes sparkle with joy and the things that blind them with tears; the things that seem to enrich and the things that seem to impoverish—"We know that all things work together for good to them that love God!" "Now unto him that is able to keep you from falling, and to present you faultless before the presence of his glory with exceeding joy, to the only wise God our Saviour, be glory and majesty, dominion and power, both now and ever. Amen."

X

PRAY FOR DELIVERANCE

"Deliver us from evil."
MATTHEW 6: 13

I

THIS IS THE PETITION OF THE LORD'S PRAYER, THE last and, to my mind, the most intensely human. It is the natural cry of conscious weakness to infinite strength. It is also the most inclusive, summing up as it does all the petitions that have gone before. Look at the bigness and breadth of it:

1. It voices a universal longing. There is not one of us that has not at some time prayed for deliverance, if not with our lips, then with our hearts. It is a prayer that is older than human history. It is as old as man. It is as old as sin and suffering and tears. But though so old, it is as new as the last item you read in the daily press. It is as new as your latest breath. It is as new as your own heartache. It is a prayer that we can never cease to pray so long as we live in this world with its sin and griefs and graves. Deliverance—that is what Adam and Eve were seeking when, in the conscious-

ness of their guilt, they hurried to hide themselves among the trees of the garden. It was the longing of the Psalmist as he held up his crimsoned hands before God and cried: "Deliver me from bloodguiltiness." It was the prayer of tortured Job as he wailed, "When shall I arise, and the night be gone?" We hear it on the lips of St. Paul as he cries, "O wretched man that I am! who shall deliver me?"

Most of you no doubt are familiar with the statue of Laocoön. It pictures a father and his two sons caught in the deadly coils of immense serpents. The faces of these strugglers are full of pain and anguish. Their muscles are astrut as they try in vain to tear from their tortured bodies the writhing monsters that are ruthlessly crushing out their lives. The suffering that looks out from their eyes, the utter hopelessness of the unequal conflict in which they are engaged, are in themselves a pathetic cry for deliverance. And as we look upon this statue we cannot but feel that it is in some measure a picture of ourselves. It symbolizes the ceaseless struggle of our race. Sometimes the fight seems as futile as that of this father and his sons. But, in spite of a million failures, it continues through all the changing centuries. Man is forever crying consciously or unconsciously, "Deliver us from evil."

2. Not only is this a prayer for all men, but it seeks deliverance from all evil. When we pray, "Deliver us from evil," we are asking for victory over every foe. This means, of course, that we are asking for

deliverance from all moral evil. It means that we are seeking freedom from sin. We are asking for clean hands and a stainless heart. We are asking for the removal of all guilt. Most of all we are praying for freedom to be and do our best. We are praying for deliverance from the fear that so often unmans us in the presence of hard and trying tasks. We are asking for deliverance from the sickening sense of impotence that so often possesses us as we face the daily demands that life makes upon us. We are praying for deliverance from the deep damnation of being spiritual dwarfs when we might be spiritual giants. When we pray this prayer, therefore, we are praying for victory over all sin.

Not only do we pray for deliverance from sin, but for deliverance from all suffering that can in any way hamper or mar our lives. We realize, of course, as others have pointed out, that not all suffering is evil. Pain and pleasure are not opposites. They are not always enemies to each other; they are sometimes close and intimate friends. For instance, I know a minister who is accustomed to suffer keenly from timidity. As he faces the prospect of appearing before a congregation he is often in positive agony. Yet this same minister finds great joy in preaching. In fact, I have known few men, I think, who experience more genuine delight in their work. What agony is that of the mother as she passes through the valley of the shadow of death to lift her child into life. Yet her suffering is no more genuine than her joy. In both these instances pleasure and pain are so mingled that it is impossible to say with certainty where the one leaves off and the other begins.

But much of the suffering we know must be reckoned as evil. Therefore, in this prayer, we are asking for deliverance from it, whether it be the evil of a pain-racked body, of a tortured mind, or of a broken heart. We are asking for victory over our worries and anxieties. We are asking for comfort in our loneliness. We are seeking for freedom from the bitterness of bereavement, from the wolf of poverty that is howling at many of our doors. We are praying for victory in the face of dreams that never come true and hopes long deferred that have made the heart sick. When we thus pray, we are asking that in all things, in all that threatens our being and doing our best, we may be conquerors and more than conquerors through him that loves us.

II

Think of the encouragement that this prayer holds for us.

1. It is encouraging because it tells us that Jesus recognizes evil as a reality. He does not look upon it as a mere illusion. He does not look upon it as good in the making. He recognizes it as a great grim fact. That does not mean, of course, that he always explains it. The Bible does not undertake to give a full explana-

tion of the presence of all the evil that is in our world. Of course it throws some valuable light upon the question. We can, for instance, understand something of the reason for the presence of moral evil. It is the result of wrong choice. In order for man to be man he must have power to choose. "A world where man would not sin would be heaven: a world where he could not sin would be hell." Man, having the power to choose, makes a wrong choice, hence there is sin.

But the reason for the evil of suffering we cannot always explain. Of course there is a type of suffering that we can easily understand. I knew a man years ago who was a member of the United States Senate. When he first came to Washington, he was a magnificent man, both physically and intellectually. Had you passed him on the street, you would doubtless have turned to look after him. He was so striking as to attract attention wherever he went. But he took to drink, and little by little liquor became his master. At last there came a day when he was as strikingly horrible as he had once been handsome. He became a tragic shadow of his former self. He suffered, and suffered terribly. But nobody looked on in amazement and asked "Why?" All knew that he was only suffering the natural consequences of his violation of the laws of health.

But not all suffering can be so easily explained. We know, of course, that sin always causes suffering. Sin never enters any life, but suffering walks at its heels.

But, while that is true, not all suffering is born directly of sin. That is where Job's three friends went wrong. They had an iron-bound theory that goodness always brings prosperity, and that suffering is a sure mark of sin. "Here," they said as they looked on Job, "is a man who is a great sufferer; he is, therefore, of necessity a great sinner." But Job knew that they were wrong. Therefore their easy reading of things made him rage. He found them more tormenting than his disease. At last he cried in desperation, "Miserable comforters are ye all." And to this indignant protest we say "Amen." For actual experience is constantly tearing the complacent theory of these comforters into shreds.

For instance, one day some men holding this conviction came to Jesus with the story of how the tower of Siloam had fallen on certain individuals and had crushed them to death. These informers were sure that the victims of this disaster must have been great sinners. They did not claim to know the particular sin of which they were guilty, but of their peculiar guilt they were sure. But Jesus told them emphatically that they were wrong, that the fact that they had been killed did not indicate in the least that they were sinners above their fellows. Why, then, did they suffer? Why was the tower allowed to fall upon them? Jesus did not undertake to answer that question. It was one of those evils that he left unexplained. But while Jesus did not always explain evil, he never denied it. While he did not explain it, he did not, as another has said, "explain it away." He faced evil as a grim fact.

2. Not only does Jesus face the fact of evil, but he takes his stand against it. When he teaches us to pray, "Deliver us from evil," he means to tell us that there is no evil in this world that is according to his will. God never inflicts evil on any man. "No harm from him can come to me, on ocean or on shore." Joseph was wise enough to see that in the long ago. He had suffered, and suffered greatly. But he refused to blame God for his suffering. He put the responsibility where it belonged, and that was upon his brothers. "Ye meant it unto me for evil," he said to them, "but God meant it unto good." What a pity that all of us do not possess his wisdom! But we are constantly blaming God for evils over which he grieves far more deeply than we. Upon this, then, we may count with assurance—that God is forever against evil.

3. Then, the fact that God is against evil is a guarantee of our final victory over it. Since he takes our side, we may be sure that we do not offer this prayer in vain. Though right does seem forever on the scaffold, and wrong forever on the throne, yet that scaffold does sway the future, and behind the dim unknown, God stands within the shadow keeping watch above his own. We may, therefore, throw ourselves into our fight against evil, whether in our own lives or in our social order, with full assurance that we do not battle for a lost and failing cause. The final victory is not

going to be with evil, but with righteousness. "Wherefore, my brethren, be ye steadfast, unmovable, always abounding in the work of the Lord, forasmuch as ye know that your labor is not in vain in the Lord."

III

Now, if God delivers us from evil, how does he do it? He does not do so by hiding us away where the rude winds that blow upon other lives cannot reach us. "I pray not," he said in his prayer of intercession for his disciples—"I pray not that thou shouldest take them out of the world, but that thou shouldest keep them from the evil." The deliverance for which we pray is not a deliverance that we have to get out of the world in order to win. It is a deliverance that it is our privilege to experience in the here and now. When we pray, then, "Deliver us from evil," what have we a right to expect?

1. Take the matter of sin—how does God deliver from sin? He breaks the fetters of those who are bound by it, and enables them to conquer where they once went down in defeat. This is the very heart of the gospel message. "The Spirit of the Lord God is upon me, because he hath anointed me to preach deliverance to the captives," was the theme of Jesus as he preached in his home church. "Who gave himself for our sins," writes Paul, "that he might deliver us from this present evil age." And that he makes good his purpose of deliverance is the testimony of an innu-

merable company that no man can number. "Who hath delivered us from the power of darkness, and hath translated us into the kingdom of his dear Son," is not theory, but experience. "Unto him that loved us and loosed us from our sins" is the testimony, not of one, but of multitudes. Christ does not bring deliverance from the bondage of sin. "He breaks the power of canceled sin, and sets the prisoner free." He takes the fluctuating son of Jonah and makes him into a rock of Christlike character. He finds Bunyan, burdened beyond endurance, and brings him within sight of the cross where his burden rolls away.

But our Lord does something even finer than that. If we only give him a chance he delivers us from sin by saving us from ever becoming its bondslaves. He takes hold of us in the sweet innocence of our youth, and keeps us to the end of the journey. Gypsy Smith tells of a testimony meeting that he attended in England years ago in his own church. A one-time drunkard told how God had saved him from the gutter. A man who had served time in prison told how he had been rescued from a life of crime. Another said that he had ridden about the city with the Lord Mayor, but had also had to beg bread from door to door. Thus one after another told his story till the Gypsy could stand it no longer. He sprang to his feet crying, "The Lord has done great things for you, but he has done far greater for me. He saved me from going astray. He has kept me from my youth." It is an amazing miracle when the prodigal is won back to the fellowship of his Father. But it is far more wonderful when he is kept from ever going into the far country. God can and does deliver us from the slavery of sin. But, better still, he delivers us from the tragedy of wasting our substance with riotous living.

2. Then, he will deliver us from the evil of suffering. Some he delivers by sparing them the tragedies that come upon certain of their fellows. Life deals far more harshly with some than with others. I have never been in the darkened rooms that some of you have been called upon to enter. There are those listening at this moment for whom every breath is a breath of pain. There are those who have had the keen disappointment of never having found a life companionship. There are those, all of whose children are dream children. There are many of life's heaviest sorrows from which the vast majority of us are spared altogether.

Then, there are those who are delivered by being rescued. Thrust into some prison of pain, they are shown a way of escape. Bound by chains of suffering as real as those that bound imprisoned Peter in the long ago, prayer is made, and their fetters fall from their hands. "I sought the Lord, and he heard me, and delivered me from all my fears." Some years ago one of the most saintly ministers that I know was hurt in an accident. Both his arms and one of his limbs were broken in three places. At one time the pain became so intense that he seemed unable to bear it.

In his agony he asked his nurse to phone certain friends of whose consecration he was sure to unite in prayer on his behalf. And account for it how you may, it is his testimony that a great peace came upon him. He fell asleep as calmly as a child upon its mother's breast. He is firm in the faith that God wrought his deliverance in answer to prayer.

But God does not always deliver after this fashion. There are times when, pray how we may, the pain remains, when the wound is not healed, when the burden is not lifted. But he delivers none the less by giving us grace and strength adequate to our needs. This, I think, is his most common way of working our deliverance, the most common and the most enriching. When Paul cried to God, for instance, for the removal of his thorn, his request was not granted. God did not take away his thorn; but he did something so much better that Paul came to rejoice that the deliverance for which he prayed was denied. Jesus asked that, if it were possible, the cup of suffering might pass from him. But God did not deliver after that fashion. He rather gave him courage and strength to drain his cup to the last drop; and thus to change the evil of the cross into infinite good.

So he is doing for some of you. In the midst of suffering, you are experiencing his daily deliverance by being made to realize that his grace is sufficient. You know how pearls are made—a grain of sand or some irritating substance gets into the shell of the oyster and inflicts a wound. In the efforts of nature to heal this wound a pearl is formed. Thus the pearl is a jewel that is born of pain. And often it is so with the most beautiful pearls of character. Here, for instance, is Robert Louis Stevenson. He is too sick to write. He is too sick to speak. Yet he dictates with his fingers, using the deaf and dumb alphabet. And he writes so sunnily and with such robust optimism that a certain critic who did not know him declared that his was entirely too joyous a reading of things, that when he had barked his shins a bit on life's grim realities he would not be so cheerful. And we forget to pity this great sufferer in our profound admiration for his courage.

Now, I wonder just what we are making of this wealthy prayer? You remember the story of how Daniel for his loyalty to his convictions was flung into the den of lions. For the king who had put him there, that night was one of great restlessness. Early next morning, therefore, this king was at the door of the den, with this question upon his lips: "O Daniel, servant of the living God, is thy God, whom thou servest continually, able to deliver thee?" And I close my message by asking this same question of your heart and mine, "Is thy God, whom thou servest, able to deliver thee?" Are you finding that the promises of God are not overstated? Are you finding Christ adequate for your needs? As you pray day by day, "Deliver us from evil," are you being delivered? "Is thy God,

whom thou servest continually, able to deliver thee?"
God grant that we may answer with the quiet assurance of this hero of the long ago, "He is able."

But if we are to make this answer, if this deliverance
is to be ours, we must share it with others. Our prayer
is not simply "Deliver me," it is "Deliver us." Years
ago I undertook the rather difficult task of rescuing a
young chap from drowning. As we fought our way to
safety, I thought more than once of giving up the task
as hopeless. He was such a heavy handicap that it
seemed at times that my efforts must end in failure.
But in our struggle for deliverance from evil, our
brother is not our handicap; he is our life preserver.
Apart from him we cannot win. "Every branch in me
that beareth not fruit he taketh away." As we pray
this prayer, therefore, we stretch a helping hand to our
friend, to our church, to our city, and to our world.

PART III
A PRAYER OF THANKSGIVING

XI

JESUS' PRAYER OF THANKSGIVING

"I thank thee, O Father, Lord of heaven and earth, because thou didst hide these things from the wise and prudent, and didst reveal them unto babes. Even so, Father: for so it seemed good in thy sight."

MATTHEW 11: 25, 26

IN THIS BRIEF AND BEAUTIFUL PRAYER JESUS PRE-sents no petition. He makes no request. He simply pours out the gratitude of his heart before his Father. Jesus doubtless often prayed after this fashion. He did so by the grave of Lazarus. With the conscious-ness that he has already won the victory in the secret place, with the assurance that he is now here in the presence of death only to receive the spoils of his con-quest, he prays, "Father, I thank thee that thou hast heard me. And I know that thou hearest me always." Jesus mastered to perfection the fine lesson that Paul urged upon his converts when he wrote, "In everything give thanks."

I

For what is Jesus thankful?

1. He is thankful for what God is doing in his own day. The God of Jesus is not merely a God of some far-off yesterday. No more is he a God of some future and hazy to-morrow. He is a present and living God, actively engaged in the here and now. Everywhere Jesus sees the prints of his marching feet. Everywhere he detects the finger-marks of his loving hands. He does not complain, therefore, with Thomas Carlyle that God is doing nothing! On the contrary he declares joyfully, "My Father worketh even until now." It is just his perception of the marvelous doings of God all about and within him that causes him to give utterance to this prayer of thanksgiving.

Not only does Jesus believe that God is present and active in his world, but he also believes that he is doing the very best possible for that world. God is doing what seems good in his sight. And for Jesus that is enough. He is sure that this leaves nothing to be desired. This does not mean, of course, that he believes that God's efforts are meeting with universal success. He knows that such is not the case. He has just pronounced sentence of doom upon certain cities that have rejected him. But he is sure that the doom pronounced is in no sense due to any lack of effort on the part of God. He is certain that God has done his loving best. We may have this same assurance in our day. But we do not always have it. There are moments, I dare say, in all our lives when we feel that if we were God we could do vastly more for this sinning and bewildered world than he is doing. But not so with Jesus. He never for a moment doubts that God is doing the best possible.

But, just what is God doing that so stirs the gratitude of Jesus? He is hiding certain things from one group and revealing them unto another. "I thank thee, O Father, Lord of heaven and earth, because thou didst hide these things from the wise and prudent, and didst reveal them unto babes." "These things!" What are "these things" that God is hiding and revealing? They are the things that matter most. They are the things of the spirit. They are things of such vast importance that if we receive them, though, if it were possible we might miss all else, life for us would be a vast victory. They are things so vital that if we fail to receive them, though, if it were possible we might win all else, life must be a pathetic and tragic failure.

"These things" include the knowledge of God and all that goes with that surpassing knowledge. Jesus is thankful that God is revealing himself to all who are willing to receive him. He is sure that there are those listening to him even now who are coming to an increasing knowledge of God. He is sadly convinced also that there are those present whose ears are becoming stopped, whose eyes are being blinded, and who are missing altogether the knowledge of those things that

belong to their peace. The same is true to-day. It will
be true of this congregation in this very hour. There
are those here present to whom God will sweetly reveal
himself. But there are others, I fear, from whom
he will hide himself behind a darker mist of gloom
and uncertainty.

Now, since "these things" include the knowledge of
God, they include also all the treasure that goes with that
priceless knowledge. Let us glance at some of this
wealth as it is set forth in the context. To find God
is to find rest. "Come unto me, all ye that labor and
are heavy laden, and I will give you rest." Those who
know God through Jesus Christ do find rest in the here
and now. For instance, they find rest from their burden of guilt. Sensitiveness to sin is not an outstanding characteristic of our day. But our lack of sensitiveness does not prove our innocence. "We have all
sinned and come short of the glory of God," whether
we ever face the fact or not. But I am confident that
there are more to-day than we commonly think who
do feel the burden of their guilt. There are those still
who can enter into sympathy with Bunyan's Pilgrim as,
with his great burden upon his back and his face turned
from his own house, he sobs, "Woe is me!" And
there are many also, thank God, who share his experience of deliverance; who like him have come within
sight of the cross where their tormenting burdens have
rolled from their weary shoulders and they have found
rest. There are those who still find an expression of a

great experience if not great poetry in that familiar hymn:

"At the cross, at the cross, where I first saw the light,
And the burden of my heart rolled away."

Then Jesus, by revealing God, brings us rest from the burden of ourselves. You remember in the *Arabian Nights,* how the "Old Man of the Sea" mounted upon the shoulders of one who sought to do him a favor. But when the time came to dismount, he refused. His poor victim had no way of dislodging him. He was therefore doomed to stagger under the weight of a galling burden. Now, "The Old Man of the Sea" for you and me is none other than our own selves. I know of no more weighty burden. I know of no more fruitful source of restlessness and wretchedness than plain, everyday selfishness. But, God through Christ works our deliverance. He gives us leisure from ourselves. The man whose self-centeredness has died under the stroke of the cross is one possessed of inward rest and peace.

Finally, Jesus gives us rest from the burden of our anxieties and our fears. How many worried and anxious and fearful people we meet to-day! A few summers ago I spent several nights alone in a large, ramshackled, old house. Sometimes I would wake in the night and hear strange noises. In fact, I soon found that I could have my noises made to order. All I had to do was to think of any kind of enemy and at once

I could hear his stealthy step. And there are those who live their whole lives in this fashion. They are constantly dogged by nagging fears. But it need not be so. It is our privilege to sing with the Psalmists: "God is our refuge and strength, a very present help in trouble. Therefore will we not fear, though the earth be moved, and though the mountains be carried into the midst of the sea." This, then, is some of the treasure that is included in the "these things" that God was revealing to some and hiding from others. And you can readily see that they are things of supreme worth.

II

Let us look next at those from whom this spiritual wealth is hidden. There are some who failed to possess their possessions. Who are they? The answer seems most amazing—Listen again to this prayer. "I thank thee, O Father, Lord of heaven and earth, because thou didst hide these things from the wise and prudent." There you have it, the wise and prudent— that is, the intelligent and understanding. How astounding! They are the very ones that we should have thought would have been the quickest to receive these things. They are at once keen and cultured. They are able to put two and two together and to reason things out. But with all their acuteness of vision they see nothing. How are we to explain this bewildering fact? Does that mean that Christianity is a religion that appeals only to the stupid and the mentally unfurnished? There are those who like to think so. But when we turn the pages of Church history, we find this easy assumption flatly contradicted. We find, of course, among the ranks of the saints, multitudes of mediocre ability. For this we devoutly thank God. But we also find among them some of the best intellects of all time. If there are nameless plodders, there are also men of genius. To presume, therefore, that ignorance and stupidity are passports into the Kingdom is to miss what Jesus means altogether.

Why, then, are these things hidden from the wise and prudent? It is not their superior wisdom that shuts the door in their faces. It is rather the pride and self-sufficiency growing out of their real or fancied possession of wisdom. Conceit does block the road to a knowledge of God. But this need not surprise us. For this holds good not only in matters of religion, but everywhere else. Some of you are teachers. Who, let me ask, is the most difficult pupil with whom you have to deal? It is not, as a rule, the one who is exceptionally brilliant, or exceptionally dull, or only mediocre. It is the pupil who was born educated, the one who already knows. Whatever may be your work, if you fancy that you know all that there is to know about it, if you are sure that you have arrived, then you will never learn any more. All further progress for you is impossible.

Jesus once told the story of a certain man, very de-

cent and respectable, who went into the temple to pray.
He stood and prayed thus with himself: "God, I thank
Thee that I am not as other men, extortioners, unjust,
adulterers. I fast twice in the week. I give tithes of
all that I possess." Here surely is one of the wise and
understanding. He has arrived. He asks God for
nothing because he feels no sense of need. His own
goodness satisfies him as completely as full barns satisfied the Rich Fool. Is God to blame because he gives
nothing? Not in the least. It is impossible for God
to give what we refuse to take or to reveal what we
refuse to see.

When Jesus says, therefore, that God hid these
things from the wise and prudent, he means that he
hid them only because they themselves refused to see.
If you should take a fish from the Mammoth Cave,
you would find it to be as blind as a stone. Why? Not
because God in his anger cursed it into blindness. The
reason rather is this—by living in the dark and refusing
to see, it has lost its capacity to see. "And Jesus beheld the city, and wept over it, saying, If thou hadst
known, even thou, at least in this thy day, the things
which belong unto thy peace! but now they are hid
from thine eyes." They were hid, not because God
had made no effort to reveal them. They were hid, not
because he had ceased to love them. They were hid
because through their own fancied wisdom and pru-
dence they had blinded their eyes and plunged themselves into the dark.

III

Then, who are these fortunate souls that see the things that God is revealing? They are the babes. This means, literally, the unspeaking. They are the youthful, the boys and the girls. Of course Jesus does not mean by this to affirm that none but children can be saved. But what he does mean, and what he emphatically asserts elsewhere, is that the door into the Kingdom is open only to children and to those who succeed by the good grace of God in becoming like children. "And they brought young children to him, that he should touch them: and the disciples rebuked those who brought them. But when Jesus saw it, he was much displeased, and said unto them, Suffer the little children to come unto me, and forbid them not: for of such is the kingdom of God. Verily I say unto you, Whosoever shall not receive the kingdom of God as a little child, he shall not enter therein." Only the childlike can become Christians. Therefore, it is far easier for a child to enter into the Life than it is for an adult. This is true for the very simple reason that it is easier to be childlike when one is a child than it is when one has left childhood years behind.

Now, why do the childlike arrive while the wise and prudent fail? For the simple reason that the child possesses by nature the characteristics that go into the making of a Christian. One of these, and the only one I shall mention here, is humility. "Whosoever therefore shall humble himself as this little child, the same is greatest in the kingdom of heaven." The door opens naturally before the humble, just as naturally as it closes before the proud and self-sufficient. But what is humility? It is certainly a virtue greatly to be coveted. Yet we do not, as a rule, look upon it with longing eyes. In fact, vast numbers are thoroughly afraid of it. This is the case, I think, because we so often fail to understand just what it is. We so readily confuse the counterfeit with the genuine. There are those, for instance, who fancy themselves humble because they are possessed of an inferiority complex. There are others who believe that humility consists in saying disparaging things about themselves that they themselves do not quite believe.

Where, then, shall we turn for an answer to our question? Naturally we turn to Jesus himself. In him we discover humility in the superlative degree. It was the one virtue in himself to which he calls attention. "Learn of me," he says. Then he gives the reason for our accepting this invitation. And the reason he gives is not the one that we should naturally expect. He does not say, "Learn of me, because I am the Only Begotten of the Father." Nor does he say, "Learn of me, because I laid the foundations of the earth and the heavens are the work of my fingers." No more does he say, "Learn of me, because in me dwelleth all the treasures of the wisdom and knowledge." He rather says, "Learn of me, because I am meek and lowly in heart. . . . Learn of me, because **I** am humble." And when we sit at his feet what does he teach us? We do not hear him speaking words of self-disparagement. He is rather making assertions about himself that no other man ever dared make. "I am the Bread of Life. He that cometh to me shall never hunger, and he that believeth on me shall never thirst. . . . I am the Light of the world. He that followeth me shall not walk in darkness. . . . I am the Resurrection and the Life. . . . I and the Father are one. . . . He that hath seen me hath seen the Father." Humility, then, certainly does not consist in thinking meanly of one's self. It rather consists, as another has pointed out, in a beautiful self-forget-fulness.

Now, this humility is natural to the unspoiled child. The wise and prudent are full of pride of intellect. They are slow to confess their ignorance. They must be sure of the position of their teacher. They will not be taken in by a mere working man. They would rather ask knowingly, "Is not this the Carpenter?" But the child is utterly free from such pride. He does not hesitate to confess his ignorance. This he does, oftentimes, by asking, to our annoyance, far more questions than we can answer. The wise and prudent are full of pride of wealth and position. They tend to fawn upon those who are above them, and to despise those whom they fancy to be beneath them. But the child is equally at home with a pickaninny or a prince.

The wise and prudent often blush even for those whom they love if they seem to them inferior. But a child is not in the least ashamed to be loyal to the one whom he loves, however lowly that one may be.

Some years ago I was walking down the streets of a Western city when I discovered a little girl with her face pressed against a forbidding wall, sobbing as though her heart would break. I could not pass her by. I asked her what the matter was. She turned her tear-wet face up to mine and said, "I have lost my daddy." "Come," I said, with cheerful confidence, "and I will help you find him." And taking her hand in mine we walked for blocks. Not finding him, we turned and went back the way we had come. Suddenly she let go my hand, leaped out into the open street, and ran at the top of her speed. I lost her for a moment. A little later I found her with her arms round a dirty, half-drunken man, and her face buried in his soiled shirt front. And when I came up, she said with un-blushing joy, "I have found my daddy." I should have been ashamed of him, but she was not ashamed. She thought not of herself, but of her father. A like hu-mility in ourselves would make us all saints.

No wonder, then, that Jesus thanks God for hiding these things from the wise and prudent, and revealing them unto babes. It only means that he is thankful that God has put the knowledge that is of supreme worth alike within reach of all. He lays down no in-telligence test. It has been well said that we must accept the vast majority of our knowledge second-hand. I am told, for instance, that certain stars are so many millions of light-years from the earth. But I cannot speak with authority. I have no first-hand knowledge of the matter. I must take my astronomy from the astronomers, my science from the scientists. But however limited my abilities, I may know God at first hand. I may say out of my own experience, "It is a true saying, and worthy of universal acceptance, that Christ Jesus came into the world to save sinners." Therefore, I can join with Jesus in this winsome prayer, "I thank thee, O Father, Lord of heaven and earth, because thou didst hide these things from the wise and prudent, and didst reveal them unto babes. Even so, Father: for so it seemed good in thy sight."

PART IV
JESUS PRAYING WITH HIS DISCIPLES

XII

JESUS PRAYING FOR HIMSELF

"Father, . . . glorify thy Son."
JOHN 17: 1

THE SCENE TO WHICH THIS TEXT INTRODUCES US IS
about the most tenderly touching in all the Bible.
Jesus is at prayer with his disciples. Kneeling about him
are those faulty but devoted men whom he counts as
his mother and brothers and sisters. This is, therefore, family prayer. They have doubtless prayed thus
many times before. But there is an added solemnity
and pathos here, because this is the last time that they
will ever pray together on this side of the grave. Their
Master is going away. They have reached the place
where the good-byes are to be said, and the heavy
shadow of that separation is resting darkly upon them.
How desperately they need this hour of prayer! And
we, too, need it. Therefore, since we dare count ourselves a part of God's family, let us draw near with
reverent expectancy and humbly bow in heart with
these as they pray together in that upper room.

I

The first petition that Jesus offers is for himself. There are those who seem to think it selfish for us to pray for ourselves. At times it is. But such is not always the case. Throughout the Scriptures we are encouraged to pray for ourselves. We read of a certain blind beggar who found his way out of darkness into radiant day by praying, not for all Israel, but by crying with cracked and strident voice, "Jesus, thou Son of David, have mercy on me." And another man who was an outcast went down to his house with a great peace in his heart because he prayed, "God be merciful to me a sinner." We are encouraged thus to pray by the example of Jesus himself. That is a wise and beautiful prayer that begins:

> "Help me to live from day to day,
> In such a self-forgetful way,
> That even when I kneel to pray,
> My prayer shall be for others."

But there are times when the best way to pray for others is to pray for one's self.

But, while the Bible encourages us to pray for ourselves, it never encourages selfish praying. There are two kinds of people, James tells us, that must forever remain spiritual pygmies. There are two classes that never arrive—that never realize their possibilities. One class is made up of those who neglect prayer altogether. "You have not," he said, looking at certain empty-handed and empty-hearted folks, "because you ask not

You are in dire poverty when you might be rich, simply because you do not pray." To the other group he said, "You ask, and receive not, because you ask amiss, that you may consume it upon your lusts. When you pray for peace, you are merely seeking for your own enjoyment. When you pray for power, you are only asking that you may occupy a position of prominence, and that your name may be often on the lips of your fellows. Unoffered prayer and selfish prayer," he tells us, "both spell spiritual poverty."

But when Jesus prayed for himself, he did not pray selfishly. When he prayed for himself, he was looking toward the glory of God and the salvation of men. This is evident as we study this petition that he here offers on his own behalf. For what is Jesus asking? "Father, glorify thy Son." And we understand what he means by the glorification of himself when he repeats and elaborates this petition a little later, as he does in the fifth verse, "And now, O Father, glorify thou me with thine own self with the glory which I had with thee before the world was." Jesus is here praying for the privilege of returning to the Father, of occupying the same position that he occupied before the incarnation, infinite ages before the morning stars sang together and all the sons of God shouted for joy.

Of course, in presenting this petition to his Father he is asking for, and accepting, all that is involved in his glorification. He is aware by what tragic roadway he is to return to the Father. He knows that his way to glorification is the way of the cross. That is how Paul understood it in later days. After telling how Jesus became obedient unto death, even the death on the cross, he goes on to say, "Wherefore God also hath highly exalted him, and given him a name which is above every name." When Jesus, therefore, prays this prayer, he prays it with glad acceptance of all that is involved in Gethsemane and Calvary. He prays it with a willingness that he as a corn of wheat shall fall into the ground and die.

But, while Jesus recognizes the fact that his way to glory leads through the valley of the shadow of death, naturally he does not for a moment believe that it ends there. For him the grave is not a terminus, but a thoroughfare. If, when he prays, "Glorify thy Son," he is looking forward to Friday with its black darkness, he is also looking forward to Easter morning with all its deathless hopes. If he is looking forward to death and accepting it, he is also looking forward to and claiming the resurrection whereby he shall "abolish death and bring life and immortality to light through the gospel." In view of all this, therefore, it is not surprising that he earnestly prays in this solemn hour: "Father, glorify thy Son."

II

Having offered this prayer for his own glorification, he gives certain reasons why his petition should be granted. This is our privilege when we pray. God, in his condescending love, invites us to exercise such boldness. "Come," he says, "and let us reason together." The husband and wife who know how to talk things over and to reason together are apt to have the most beautiful and satisfying marriage relationship. The father who is wisest in dealing with his son will do more than command. He will invite his son to reason with him. And thus our Father, who is infinitely wise and tender, invites us to reason with him. When we pray, therefore, we may, as our Master, give reasons why our prayers should be answered.

What reasons does Jesus give for the answering of his prayer for glorification?

1. The time has come for that great event. "Father," he prays, "the hour is come; glorify thy Son." John always represents Jesus as running according to schedule. This schedule, to which he had strict regard, was not made out by himself, but by his Father. He lived his life completely within the will of God. For instance, when, at Cana, Mary came saying, "They have no wine," Jesus answered: "Woman, what have I to do with thee? mine hour is not yet come"—thus indicating that henceforth the finger that will point to the hour at which he will act will be that of no human hand, but of the Father. Again, he said to his brothers: "I go not yet up unto this feast; for my time is not yet full come." But now, the hour for his glorification has struck. Therefore, with confidence, he offers this prayer: "Glorify thy Son."

2. The second reason Jesus gives for the granting of his request is that his mission in this world has been fulfilled. "I have glorified thee on the earth, having finished the work which thou gavest me to do." He has come into the world for the doing of a definite task. That task is now completed. For when Jesus declares, "I have finished the work which thou gavest me to do," he does not mean simply that he has reached the end of his earthly journey. We all do that. He rather means that he has perfectly fulfilled the will of God, that his life is a completed life, that he has written no word that needs to be erased, that he has omitted none that needs to be inserted. Therefore, since his work here is finished, it is only reasonable that he should return to his Father.

3. The final reason that Jesus gives for the granting of this petition is that it is for the glory of God. "Father," he prays, "glorify thy Son, that thy Son also may glorify thee." What has the Son been doing ever since his incarnation? He has been glorifying God. That is what he dares to say to the Father as he prays this prayer, "I have glorified thee on the earth. Since I have glorified thee here by finishing the work that thou gavest me to do, and since I would continue to glorify thee throughout eternity, and since I can now best do this in thine immediate presence, therefore take me to be with thyself." It is a reasonable prayer, one to which he is sure his Father must attend.

III

Now, how does Jesus through his glorification expect to glorify the Father? He expects to glorify him by continuing the work that he has begun during the days of his flesh. When Jesus ascended to be with the Father, he did not change his purpose. He still marches toward the same goal to which he marched when he plodded the dusty highways of Judea and Galilee. What he was doing then, he is doing still. Luke calls attention to this fact in the opening words of the Book of Acts. "The former treatise have I made, O Theophilus, of all that Jesus began both to do and teach, until the day in which he was taken up." He begins in the realm of the seen; he continues in the realm of the unseen.

Now, what did Jesus do and teach as a beginning? Why did the Word become flesh and dwell among us? He puts it in a single sentence when he declares, "The thief cometh not, but for to steal, and to kill, and to destroy: I am come that they might have life, and that they might have it more abundantly." His gift to every man that would take it was the gift of eternal life. Some were unwilling to receive it. That was one of the great surprises of his ministry. He watched the multitudes as they hurried by in mad pursuit of varied nothings, and cried after them with words that are still wet with tears, "Ye will not come to me, that ye might have life."

But though there were those that refused his gift, it

was hard for any to fail to recognize that he himself possessed what he so eagerly offered to others. When we seek for the secret of the spell that Jesus cast over men, we find it, at least in part, to be this: His was the spell of one who was tremendously alive. One day a young man of wealth and position ran down the road to kneel at his feet. This man was an aristocrat, and the One at whose feet he kneeled was, in the eyes of the best people of that day, a mere social nobody. Yet this young man forgets all this, as, with a face the very embodiment of wistfulness, he flings himself at the Master's feet. Why does he do it? He feels that this young rabbi has life, and he wants to know his secret. "What shall I do to inherit eternal life?" he asks. "I want life that is good to-day, that will be good to-morrow, that will outlast the world—life that will walk with me through the eternities. Tell me how to get it, for I am sure you know."

On another day, Jesus is preaching to a vast and enthusiastic audience. But he did not get far into his sermon before the enthusiasm began to chill. The crowd grew restless. Then they began to drift away in groups of tens and scores and hundreds, saying as they walked away, "He is a bit fanatical, a little mad. Really, his family ought to look after him." At first those straggling groups on the outskirts of the crowd were not missed. But soon those nearer to the speaker were going, and then others, then others still. At last there were less than a thousand, then less than five hundred, then less than a hundred, then only twelve. And these were looking over their shoulders with frightened eyes, wondering if they had not better go too. Then Jesus arrested them with this question: "Will ye also go away?" And Peter, who said a good many foolish things, pulled himself together and said something that was really magnificent. Stepping a little closer to his Lord, he said, "Master, I am ashamed to say that I was on the point of running. Possibly I would go yet, but there is really nowhere to go. To whom shall we go but unto thee? Thou hast the sayings of life." The purpose of Jesus in the world, then, was to give men life.

But, what is the life that he gives? He speaks of it as "eternal life." What is it to have life eternal? What was Bunyan's pilgrim seeking when he put his fingers in his ears and set out running, crying, "Life! Life! Eternal Life!" He was not seeking eternal existence, but eternal right existence. And how do we get hold on that? Hear the answer from the lips of our Lord: "This is life eternal, that they might know thee the only true God, and Jesus Christ whom thou hast sent." Jesus gave men eternal life while he was here, and gives men eternal life still, by enabling them to know God. Whoever knows God through Christ is in possession of eternal life.

Those who came to know Jesus when he was here were thoroughly convinced of this fact. Those men who came closest to him, who lived with him day by day, were absolutely sure that through knowing him they had come to know God. It was out of his own experience that John wrote, "No man hath seen God at any time. But the only begotten Son who is in the bosom of the Father, he hath declared him." And those who discovered God in him were only making the discovery that Jesus intended that they should make. He was pained and surprised when they made any other discovery.

For instance, during this conversation in the upper room Philip prayed a very human prayer. It was, also, a tremendously big and worthful prayer. But Jesus was not pleased with it. He was rather disappointed. "Lord," said Philip, "show us the Father, and it is enough." Of course nobody could ask for anything bigger than that. But Jesus turned with tenderness, touched with grief, and said, "Have I been so long time with you, and yet hast thou not known me, Philip? he that hath seen me hath seen the Father." How we rejoice in that answer! For infinitely the best that we can ask even of God is that he be like Jesus. To know Jesus, then, is to know God, and to know God is to have eternal life.

Now, since Jesus gave men life eternal while he dwelt among them by enabling them to know God, he is going to continue to do this after his glorification. But, if so, how? I do not wonder that these disciples of his were greatly perplexed. I do not wonder that when they became sure of his going away they felt

that their whole world had collapsed. I am not surprised that the shadows were very black about them
as they thought of the long, empty, gray days ahead,
when Jesus should no longer be at their side. In the
old days they had felt the touch of his hand. They
had heard the sound of his voice. They had looked
into his calm and kindly eyes. How would they get on
and do his work when he was gone? Peter was speaking out of his very heart when he declared that he was
ready to go with him to prison and to death. He was
sure that life would not be worth living without him.

And does not a visible Christ whom we can touch,
and who can touch us, who can hear our voices, and
whose voice we can hear, appeal to us still? You are
looking forward to some dark crisis, maybe some
difficult operation, where the physician holds out but
little hope. What would it mean to have him walk by
your side down the hallway of the hospital and into
the operating room? What would you give to have
him hold your hand as you slip out into unconscious-
ness? What would it mean to have him thus during
that harder ordeal when the sufferer was not yourself,
but one dearer than life? We older children can sometimes sing, with far greater fervor than those who
are young, this children's hymn:

"I think when I read that sweet story of old,
    When Jesus was here among men,
How he called little children as lambs to his fold,
    I should like to have been with him then.

I wish that his hands had been placed on my head,
    That his arms had been thrown around me,
That I might have seen his kind look when he said,
    Let the little ones come unto me."

Jesus knew just how these sorrowing friends of his were feeling about his going. That is the reason he said just before offering this prayer: "It is expedient for you that I go away: for if I go not away, the Comforter will not come unto you; but if I depart, I will send him unto you." "My going away," he declares in words of unspeakable comfort, "does not mean that you are to be left orphans. It does not mean that you are going to have your eyes blinded by tears as you long for the touch of a vanished hand, and the sound of a voice that is still. I am going away only that I may come the nearer to you. Up to this time I have only been with you. After I am glorified I will not only be with you, but I will be within you."

Jesus was speaking to the same purpose when "in the last day, that great day of the feast, he stood and cried, saying, If any man thirst, let him come unto me, and drink. He that believeth on me, as the Scripture hath said, out of his inner life shall flow rivers of living water. But this spake he of the Spirit, which they that believe on him were to receive: for the Holy Spirit was not yet given; because that Jesus was not yet glorified." The glorification of Christ must precede the coming of the Spirit. Therefore, when Christ prayed, "Glorify thy Son," he was praying, not that he should ascend into heaven and be separated from men, but rather that, by ascending, he should come infinitely closer to men. Coming thus to live in your heart and mine, he glorifies God in our personal lives. And not only so, but he glorifies him through our lives, for the life indwelt of God through the Spirit has a divine overflow. "Out of his inner life shall flow rivers of living water."

I am told that a few years ago a young man from America who was a genuinely winsome Christian secured a position in one of the government schools of Japan. Naturally he was forbidden to teach his faith in this school supported by the state. He had to pledge himself to that effect, and he was scrupulously loyal to his promise. Yet before the year was ended some forty of the students who had attended his classes met and pledged their allegiance to the Christ whom he had not mentioned. This was the case because out of his inner life were flowing rivers of living water that made "the wilderness and the solitary place to become glad, and the desert to rejoice and blossom as the rose!" When Jesus prayed, therefore, for his own glorification, he was asking for God's best for you and for me and for the whole world.

XIII

JESUS PRAYING FOR OUR KEEPING

*"Holy Father, keep through thine
own name those whom thou hast
given me, that they may be one, as
.we are."*

JOHN 17: 11

ONCE MORE WE ARE IN THE UPPER ROOM WHERE
the atmosphere is sweet with the breath of
prayer. Once more we are privileged to kneel with
those of the long ago as their Master and ours leads us
to the throne of grace. Again we hear Jesus praying
for himself: "Father, glorify thy Son, that thy Son
also may glorify thee: as thou hast given him power
over all flesh, that he should give eternal life to as
many as thou hast given him. And this is life eternal,
that they might know thee the only true God, and Jesus
Christ whom thou hast sent. I have glorified thee on
the earth: I have finished the work which thou gavest
me to do. And now, Father, glorify thou me with
thine own self with the glory which I had with thee
before the world was."

Having prayed for himself, he proceeds to pray for
his own: "I pray for them: I pray not for the world,

but for them which thou hast given me. . . . Neither
pray I for these alone, but for them also which shall
believe on me through their word." Thus he remem-
bers you and me, and all his own. It is a great privilege to have any saint call our names in the audience
chamber of the King. Surely Tennyson was right in
saying that more things are wrought by prayer than
this world dreams of. How often we receive new
strength, how often we are comforted because somebody is praying for us! More than once have our lips
been anointed with grace and power, because some
saint of God was pleading our needs in the secret
place of the Most High. It is a privilege, I repeat, to
be remembered in prayer even by the least of the
saints. What a privilege unspeakable to be remembered
by Jesus himself!

Now, what does Jesus ask for those who are kneeling
about him? What request does he make for these
sorrowing souls who are bowed under the weight of
the tragedy of the coming separation?

Jesus makes it plain that he is not asking for them
what he has just asked for himself. He has just reminded the Father that his work here is done, and
has therefore requested that he be taken out of the
world. That is possibly what these devoted friends
are expecting him to ask for themselves. No doubt
there are some among them that are sincerely hoping
that he will pray for this. Had not Peter just asked
with an ache in his heart and a sob in his throat, "Lord,

why cannot I follow thee now? I am ready to go with thee, both into prison, and to death." But regardless of their expectations or desires he makes no such request. On the contrary he begins his petition after this fashion: "I pray not that thou shouldest take them out of the world."

By this, the Master indicates that his whole program does not consist in merely getting folks out of this world into another and a better. Many of our fathers thought that the one purpose of our Lord was to get men and women into heaven. Now, he truly longs to do that. To that end he prays before he finishes his prayer. But that is not his sole purpose. He not only has a program for the life to come, but for the life that now is. It is not only the purpose of Jesus to get us into heaven by and by, but to get heaven into us in the here and now. We need to bear both these facts in mind. Not that we of to-day have any tendency to go to extremes in "otherworldliness." We rather tend to go in the opposite direction. Our generation seems to have largely lost its faith in a future life. And that loss prevents us from making the best out of the life that now is. This is true because the little space between the cradle and the grave, with nothing beyond, is too cribbed, cabined, and confined to call out the best in us.

But, if Jesus does not pray for their removal from the world, for what, I repeat, does he pray? He prays that they may be kept by the power of God. "Holy

Father, keep in thine own name those whom thou hast given me." He takes this little group that he loves to the uttermost, and puts them into his Father's hands. It is said that years ago a vessel went down off the coast of California. There were not enough life boats, and many were left to perish. But there was a mother who saw to it that her laddie, a little fellow some eight years of age, had a place among the rescued, though she herself had to be left behind. As she told the little chap good-by, she gave him this message to his father who was waiting for him in San Francisco: "Tell him that your mother loved you well enough to die for you, and that he must keep you with tenderest care." And thus Jesus, as he puts these into his Father's hands, prays, "Holy Father, keep them."

II

What is the content of this keeping that Jesus asks for his own?

He is not asking that they may have an easy time; he does not pray so foolishly for his children as we sometimes pray for ours. I was talking to a mother some time ago about her boys. She expressed a most fervent hope that not one of them would enter a certain field where the sacrifices are many, but the rewards great. "Why," I asked, "are you so against your sons entering upon this high calling?" "Because I do not wish them to have a hard time," was the reply. She wanted them to get through the world with as flabby muscles and as soft palms as possible. But Christ makes no such mistake in praying for these that are so dear to him. He does not ask that they be exempt from conflicts, from suffering, from desperate battles and sore wounds.

Now, since this is the case, since his supreme ambition for them is not that they shall have an easy life, he does not ask for them a quiet cloister. He does not plead that they may be kept "far from the madding crowd's ignoble strife." He himself lived his life in the thick of things. The multitudes thronged him. He was elbowed by all sorts of nameless and needy souls. He was a friend of publicans and sinners. He moved constantly where cross the crowded ways of life. Naturally he felt that it is enough for the servant that he be as his Lord. Therefore, he does not ask for these disciples a way of escape from the world; he rather asks that they may remain in the world, kept by the power of God.

And that, we may be sure, is his will for you and me. I read somewhere of a certain monk who recently came into one of our great cities, boasting of the fact that he had not been in the world before for a quarter of a century. He had been hidden away, the writer said, preening himself, getting himself ready to fly. But the world would rot down if every Christian were like that. It is in the world where need is. It is in the world where there is heartache. It is in the world that there are wounds that we must heal. There was a great hue and cry a few years ago about the preacher in politics. But where there is corruption, where there is wrong, where there is injustice, there the preacher must be, there every disciple must be, who would follow his Lord.

What, then, is this keeping for which Jesus prays? It looks in two directions. It is both negative and positive. He prays that they may be kept from something. He believes that there is something that men desperately need to be saved from. He prays also that they may be kept to something. He believes with equal conviction that there is something that men must be saved to.

1. Look first at the negative side: "I pray not that thou shouldest take them out of the world, but that thou shouldest keep them from the evil, or the evil one." Jesus is praying that these disciples of his may be kept clean from all stain of sin. It is evidently his faith that God is able, in this present world, to make them conquerors and more than conquerors through him who loves them. He is praying that they may be "a glorious church without spot or blemish or any such thing." And what he longs for in them, he longs for in us. And I am confident that we are not emphasizing our possible victory over sin to-day as he would have us do.

2. Then he prays, "Holy Father, keep them in thy name, that they may be one." Here he asks that they may be kept true to God as he has revealed him, that

they may be kept in love and loyalty to the Father. Of course it is only by this positive keeping that they can be saved from evil. The man out of whom the unclean spirit had gone was cleansed from evil, but his hands and his heart were empty, and this emptiness invited occupation. Therefore, there entered in seven other spirits and made the last state of this man worse than the first. It is only by positive loyalty to God that we can conquer. "This I say, Walk in the Spirit, and ye shall not fulfill the lust of the flesh."

Not only does Jesus pray that these be kept in loyalty and love to God, but also to each other. He reckons them as a brotherhood. Through their common love to God, and through their love to one another, they have become one. He prays, therefore, that they may continue to love each other in order that they may continue to be one. Their love is to be their distinguishing characteristic. "By this shall all men know that ye are my disciples, if ye have love one to another."

III

Then, just as when he prayed for himself, the Master gives certain reasons why his request for their keeping should be granted.

1. The Father should keep them because they are in desperate need of his keeping. They need this for two reasons. First, they are alone since he himself is no longer with them. "While I was with them in the

world, I kept them in thy name," he declares. That is, "the fact that they are thine to-day, the fact that they are one in faith and one in heart, is because of my constant watch-care of them. I have been their Friend, their Shepherd. I have been their constant keeper. They have no sufficient strength in themselves. They are what they are to-day because of my keeping. If they continue to fight the good fight, they must, in the future, be kept by thee."

But, not only do they need keeping because they must now walk alone so far as the visible presence of their Lord is concerned, but because they must walk alone in a hostile world. Jesus never counted upon the friendship of this world. "He was in the world, and the world was made by him, and the world knew him not." His unworldliness made him unpopular. It antagonized those who were worldly. He foresaw the same kind of antagonism for his followers. "If ye were of the world, the world would love its own; but because ye are not of the world, but I have chosen you out of the world, therefore the world hateth you." We do not sing with the zestful conviction of our fathers, "Is this vile world a friend to grace to help me on to God?" We balk at the word "vile." We declare almost indignantly that this is not a vile world.

Now, if you mean by world, this visible abiding place of ours, with its hills and mountains, its lakes and rivers, its seas and stars, then I agree with you. There are times when even the blindest of us feel like singing with Browning: "Oh world, as God has made it, all is beauty." But this is not what Jesus means by the world. What is the world, and what is it to be worldly? We speak sometimes of a "worldly Christian." There really isn't any such creature. But when we speak thus of a Church member, we usually mean one who is given to the practice of certain worldly amusements, such as dancing, card-playing, theater-going. Of course one who does these things may be worldly. But others who do none of them may be equally so. To be worldly is to be dominated by the spirit that dominates the world, and that is the spirit of self-pleasing. And if greed and grab and self-seeking are vile things, this is a somewhat vile world.

But Jesus declared that he had overcome the world. By this he meant that he had overcome the love of it, and the fear of it. He had overcome its spirit of self-seeking with its worries, its prides, and its burning lusts. And he generously credits these followers of his with a like victory. "They are not of the world," he reminds the Father, "even as I am not of the world." But since they are still in the world, and since the world is always striving for the mastery, and since to surrender to it spells disaster, they greatly need the Father's keeping. No wonder, therefore, that Jesus prays, "Now I am no more in the world, but these are in the world. Holy Father, keep them."

2. The second reason that Jesus offers for the grant-ing of his request is that thereby his own name may

be glorified. He knows that it is only those who **are** kept that are able truly to glorify God. He recognizes the fact that they have a definite work to do: "As the Father hath sent me into the world, even so have I sent them into the world." They are here as the salt of the earth. They are here as the light of the world. But they can only fulfill their mission if they are kept by the power of God. This is only plain common sense. We cannot preach salvation from sin with conviction unless we are experiencing our Master's keeping in our own lives. We cannot effectively proclaim a gospel of love with our lips unless we proclaim it by our daily lives. The church whose members are kept true to God and to each other, will be a conquering church, and will thus glorify our Lord. All others will fail.

3. The final reason that Jesus gives for this keeping is this: "They are thine." "Father," he says, "these belong to thee." Since this is the case, thou art under infinite obligations to keep them. Faulty as we are, we recognize something of our obligations to our own. It is my business to make the burdens and needs of my son my own just because he is mine. This is true whether he is weak or strong, dull or brilliant, good or bad. The same is true of you in relation to your child. You shared with God in his creation. Therefore a weighty obligation rests with you that you cannot ignore.

A pastor told me some time ago of a very saintly mother who belonged to his congregation, who had a

wild and worthless son. She was such a lovable character that the Official Board, for her sake, got her son
out of trouble more than once. But, in spite of their
interest, he went from bad to worse, till he fell into
positive crime. The Board then decided that it would
only do harm to help him further. Having reached
this decision, they asked this pastor to convey their
decision to the mother. This he did, advising her at
the same time that she would do well to follow the
same course. It was then that the soul of the mother
stood up in her eyes. "Doctor," she said, "I don't
blame you and the Board in the least for the course you
have taken; you have been very kind. But his mother
can't take it. She can't give him up. Why, I gave
him life. I rocked him to sleep in these old arms
when he was a little baby. I looked the love-light in
his eyes in his young and tender years. I can't go back
on him, because he's mine."

And what Jesus is saying to his Father is this:
"These are thine, thine by creation, thine above all by
redemption." Of course God cannot keep those who
will not have his keeping any more than this mother
could keep her boy. But where God's child is willing,
then his obligations to that child are infinite. "I
pledged thee," Jesus seems to say; "I have told these
men that if they would put thee first, that if they would
seek first the kingdom of God and his righteousness,
that thou wouldst stand back of them, that thou wouldst
never let them down, never fail, nor forsake them.

Thy faithfulness demands that those who are thine by self-surrender be kept. Thou art personally responsible for them, for they are thine."

And that God does keep those who put themselves in his hands is the testimony of all the saints of all the centuries. Here is a testimony that comes out of the long ago. One day a man living amidst a rich and growing civilization received, as he believed, a definite call from God. The voice that spoke to him said, "Get thee out from thy father's house, . . . and I will bless thee, and thou shall be a blessing." And this man turned his face toward the unknown. From a dweller in a great city, he became a nomad of the desert. And the slow years slipped by till he was an old man, old and childless, and there seemed no slightest hope that his dream would come true. But Abraham never turned back. He was sure that he had heard God's voice. He counted him faithful who had promised. And of course God kept faith with him, as he always does.

Here is a testimony from to-day. A gifted young man is away at college to study law. But one day he writes home that he has decided to enter the ministry. It was a great blow to his mother, almost a heart-breaking blow. But she bore it because of necessity. Other days went by and there came another letter saying that he was not only going to preach, but going to be a foreign missionary. This was the last straw! That mother went to bed with a broken heart. Then there came a telegram urging him to come at once, that his mother was not expected to live. When he reached home, his older brother, who was a physician, took him aside and said: "There is only one chance for mother, and that is for you to tell her that you have given up all thought of being a missionary." What a test! But he did not do this. Instead, he went alone to remind God that he had put everything into his hands, and that he had pledged to see him through. And it is his testimony that God did not let him down. Instead, he raised the mother to newness of life, physically and spiritually, and made the young man himself the greatest missionary of our day. He will not fail us who are his. On the contrary he will enable us to shout with Paul, "I know whom I believe, and am persuaded that he is able to keep that which I have committed unto him against that day."

thou gavest me, I have kept, and none of them is lost,
but the son of perdition."

XIV

JESUS' PRAYER OF CONFESSION

*"While I was with them in the
world, I kept them in thy name:
those that thou gavest me I have
kept, and none of them is lost, but
the son of perdition."*

JOHN 17: 12

THIS IS A PRAYER OF CONFESSION. IT IS NOT A
confession of sin. Jesus never had to make that
tragic confession. In that he was unlike ourselves.
We must make such confession, or fail to state what is
true of every one of us. We must make it in order to
find deliverance. "If we say we have no sin, we de-
ceive ourselves, and the truth is not in us. If we
confess our sins, he is faithful and just to forgive us
our sins, and to cleanse us from all unrighteousness."
But, while Jesus has no confession of sin to make, he
does confess that in some measure he has failed. One
whom he loves with passionate and tender devotion has
slipped through his clinging fingers. With breaking
heart he has to confess that in spite of all that love and
constant care could do, he has lost him. Those that

183

thou gavest me I have kept, and none of them is lost, but the son of perdition."

Of course this text is more than a confession of failure. It has in it far more of victory than defeat. What Jesus is saying to the Father is this: "I have kept most of those whom thou hast committed to my care. I have kept impulsive and fickle Simon. In spite of many a weakness and many a blunder my grace has proved sufficient for him. I have kept James and John, the sons of thunder, in spite of their narrowness and their keen ambition. I have kept Matthew, having wooed him from his moneybags. I have kept gloomy and doubting Thomas, in spite of the fact that he tends to cling to life's somber and shady side as ivy clings about old ruins. But Judas has thwarted me. Judas has disappointed all the fine dreams that I cherished for him. In spite of all the big possibilities that were locked in his roomy heart, in spite of all that I did for him and longed to do, he has run past me and I have lost him."

Now this confession on the part of Jesus is arresting for many reasons. But our interest in it for the present is because of the vivid light that it throws on the character of Judas. What are we to think of this man who betrayed his Lord with a kiss? There are two popular literary pastimes in vogue to-day. One of them is the witty art of "de-bunking." This consists of digging certain moral and spiritual kings from their honored graves and snatching away their crowns and wrenching the scepter from their hands. Our debunker shows us that all our heroes had feet of clay, and that in honoring them we have gathered dust and dirt, not upon our knees only, but upon our souls as well. The other consists of taking some recognized scoundrel, and showing that he was a misunderstood saint or an angel in disguise. It is not surprising, therefore, that even Judas has his defenders. He was not, after all, a treacherous hater of Jesus, but a misguided enthusiast. But, what do we learn about him from our text?

I

The first fact that this text brings to our attention is that Judas once belonged to Jesus, and was, therefore, a good man. When the Master declared that he had lost him, that in itself was a declaration that Judas was once his very own. We cannot lose what we never possess. Before I can lose a fortune I must possess a fortune. Judas belonged to Jesus just as Peter and James and John and Matthew belonged to him. This is the assertion of this text, and it is in harmony with all the rest that is said of Judas in the New Testament. I am aware of course that there are those who affirm that Judas was a devil from the beginning. But the Scriptures bring no such accusation. Luke tells us, not that Judas was a traitor, but that he became a traitor. No man can become a traitor who has been one from the beginning. Peter in speaking of Judas declares that he fell. In order for any man to fall, he must first in some fashion stand upon his feet. Now since Judas once belonged to Jesus and fell into treachery we feel safe in saying that he was at one time a good man.

The one-time goodness of Judas is further indicated by the confidence that both Jesus and his disciples placed in him. When the Apostles were organized, it was Judas who was selected to be the treasurer. That indicates confidence. We are not accustomed to put our money into the hands of men whom we do not trust. Some months before the end, Jesus recognized the duplicity of Judas; but his fellow disciples trusted him to the very end. When they sat together at the last supper and Jesus said, "One of you shall betray me," they did not all turn with one accord to point accusing fingers at Judas. It never occurred to them that he was worse than themselves. But with a beautiful humility that did not always characterize them, they questioned, each for himself, "Lord, is it I?"

Finally, the goodness of Judas is indicated by the fact that he was an Apostle. Now, before he could become an Apostle, two choices had to be made. First, Judas had to choose Jesus. How came Judas to be a follower of our Lord? He followed him because he chose to follow him. The Scriptures indicate that Judas was a lover of money. This was doubtless his supreme passion before he met Jesus. But one day the Master came his way and cast his spell over him. So tremen-

dous was the appeal of Jesus that he gave up the possibility of becoming rich and forsook all to follow him.
And this he did in spite of the fact that Jesus was a
confessed son of poverty, and in spite of the further
fact that he declared that the denial of self was an absolute essential for entrance into his kingdom.

Of course it is easy to reply to all this that, while
Judas followed Jesus, he did so from mixed motives.
That Judas was a man of mixed motives I think there
is no doubt. But let him who is without that same sin
cast the first stone at him. This would doubtless forbid most of us. It would certainly make any stoning
on the part of his fellow disciples impossible. James
and John became great and good men. But one day
these came, hiding behind the skirts of their mother,
to ask for seats, the one on the right hand and the other
on the left, in his kingdom. And when their fellows
heard about it, they fairly boiled with indignation. But
their indignation was not due to the fact that James and
John were men of mixed motives; it was rather because
these two were seeking honors that they themselves
thought ought to be their own. The motives of Judas
in following Jesus, then, were doubtless not perfectly
pure. But there is no slightest indication that they
were not as pure as those of his fellow-apostles.

But not only did Judas choose Jesus; but what is
more arresting, Jesus chose Judas. This does not
mean simply that Jesus allowed him to become one of
his followers, but that he chose him as one of the inner

circle, as one of the twelve. He chose him as he did the others, after a night spent in prayer. He chose him under divine guidance. We may be sure, therefore, that he did not choose him because he misunderstood him. The Scriptures plainly assert that Jesus knew what was in man, and needed not that any should teach him. No more did Jesus choose him because he knew him to be a rascal. That is absolutely unthinkable. If he chose him to play a part in the grim tragedy of the cross, then Judas was in no sense to blame for the playing of that part. Some years ago a rather sordid and sensational play was staged in one of our Southern cities. The villain of the story was a mulatto negro. He played his part so well that he came very nearly getting mobbed. Yet he was neither a negro nor a villain, only a good actor. But Judas was just as blameless as this man if he was only chosen to play a part.

Why, then, did Jesus choose Judas? He chose him just as he chose John. He chose him because he was the best man in sight for the place. Jesus knew he was not perfect. He saw the vast possibilities for evil that were in his heart. But he also saw the vast possibilities for good. Soil that is fertile enough to grow an abundant harvest of weeds can also be made to grow an abundant harvest of wheat. Jesus saw this fertile soil in the heart of Judas, and yearned to bring it to its highest possibilities. Hence he chose him, as another has pointed out, just as he chose all the others, as a great and high adventure of faith. Therefore, from all these considerations, we must conclude that Judas was once a good man.

II

But Jesus lost Judas. It is important, therefore, to know how this tragic loss came about. When the Master confessed that he had lost this man, he did so with deep grief. But there was no sense of guilt or of shame in his confession. He knew that he had not lost him through any fault of his own. Jesus had done his loving best for Judas, as he does for every one of us. Neither had he lost Judas by blind chance or through some evil fate. He had not lost him because it was decreed before the foundation of the world that he should lose him. This expression, that the Scriptures might be fulfilled, is another way of saying that, with the result that the Scriptures were fulfilled. Jesus lost Judas because of a deliberately wrong choice. Peter lets us in to the whole secret when he declares that Judas fell through transgression.

Now this brings us onto familiar territory. Judas fell just as we may fall—through sin. He was just as human as we are. The possibilities for evil that were in his life are in ours also. We tend to forget this. As we look upon those who have gone greatly wrong, we love to feel that they are vastly different from ourselves. We love to feel that while they are made of the slime and ooze of things, we are made out of quite different and better material. But we are all close akin in that we are all sinners. And the difference between the worst of us and the best of us is in degree, rather than in kind. And if you have never discovered the possibility of a Judas in yourself, it is not so much a mark of superior goodness as of superior blindness. We have all walked the same road that Judas walked. The only difference is that in the good grace of God we have not gone quite so far.

We may be sure of this further fact that Judas went down gradually. That is always the case. No man ever reaches the highest height of sainthood at a single bound. No more does he sound the lowest depths of infamy. We ascend into heaven, or we descend unto hell, a step at a time. Mr. Hyde does not gain the mastery over Dr. Jekyll in one single conflict. It is a process that covers a period of weeks and months and years. So it was with Judas. One day, instructed to give a certain sum to the poor, he withheld a few pennies. "It is not stealing," he told himself; "it is just legitimate salary. Have I not had all the worry of handling the funds? Besides, I am going to pay it back later on." But he never paid it back. Instead, he took a little more. And each time, with less outrage to his conscience and less thought of restitution.

Now, this dishonesty began at once to tell upon his relationship to his Master. He was perfectly sure that Jesus knew him for what he was. This began to make him increasingly wretched and resentful. More and more everything that Jesus said that could possibly be taken as a rebuke was so construed. "Take heed, and beware of covetousness," Jesus doubtless said more than once; "for a man's life consisteth not in the abundance of the things which he possesseth." To Judas honest, this seemed the height of good sense; but to Judas dishonest and disintegrating, it was a reproof that made him grind his teeth with rage. For when we are rebuked for our sin, we usually take one of two courses—we either come to hate the sin for which we are rebuked, or to hate the one who rebukes us. (When the physician tells us that we are suffering from some deadly malady, we either take the side of the physician against the disease, or the side of the disease against the physician.) Judas came little by little to take the latter course. Naturally, therefore, from a lover of Jesus he was changed into a hater.

Toward the end, Jesus said to Judas, "Have not I chosen you twelve, and one of you is a devil?" But even then Jesus did not dismiss Judas. He still clung to him, hoped for him, sought to win him. We often say of certain failing and sinning individuals that they ought to be turned out of the Church. But Jesus seems not to have regarded this as a remedy. He did not believe that ostracism could be depended upon to accomplish results greater than love. And experience indicates his wisdom. Years ago there was a man in my church who was conspicuous for his generosity. He was the father of twelve children, all of whom were at home. In spite of this fact, however, he adopted four others. But he had one great weakness. Now and then he would get beastly drunk. Naturally there were those who were outraged by such conduct, and thought we ought to shut the door of the church in his face. But there were others who did not feel that this was the best way to save either him or his family. By and by, he had a lovely daughter to volunteer for the mission field. At first he was in bitter rebellion against it. But at last he gave his consent. Not only so, but he came into a deep and beautiful religious experience. Since then I am told he has walked in newness of life. And the church had won through love.

But love is not always victorious. Though Jesus clung to Judas to the end, he had at last to confess that he had lost him. It was Judas who led the soldiers and the mob to his place of prayer one night and said, "Hail, Master," and kissed him. A terrible and perplexing thing—this kiss! Jesus himself seemed fairly startled by it. He knew there was no love in it, but hate and contempt. He knew that this was not merely misguided enthusiasm. There are those who claim that Judas really loved Jesus, and was only doing this to compel him to assert himself. But Jesus knew it was treachery. "Betrayest thou the Son of man with a kiss?" he asked. Judas did not through misguided enthusiasm do a foolish thing. He rather through treachery did a damnable thing.

III

In what sense did Jesus lose Judas? A mother showed me a picture of a lovely child some time ago. As we looked at it, she said with tender sorrow, "He stayed with us only a few short years, and then we lost him." She meant, of course, that the little boy had died. But she was using the wrong word. She had not really lost him. The Christ of little children had merely taken him up in his arms and put his hands upon him and blessed him. He was keeping her treasure safe for her in the house of many mansions. It was not in this sense that Jesus lost Judas. Another mother was sitting down to dinner with her family the other night, when a catcall whistle came from out the dark. At once her oldest son, a boy of about sixteen, pushed his chair back from the table and made for the door. The mother clung to him for a brief minute, pleading with him not to go. But he flung her hand from his shoulder, and hurried out into the night. Then she burst into tears and said, "I have lost him!" That was far nearer the truth than the declaration of the other mother.

Now, that is in part the meaning of Jesus' loss of Judas. Jesus lost him in that Judas ceased to love and trust him. In fact, his love changed to hate, and his faith died utterly. Therefore, when the darkest hour of his life came upon him, he turned not to Jesus, but to his enemies. It is impossible to look upon Judas in this tragic hour without profound pity. After his treacherous kiss had been given, and his Master had been led away, he felt something in his bosom that burned like live coals. It was the thirty pieces of silver. He must be rid of it at all costs. So he hurried to those who had duped him, and flung it down at their feet, saying, "I have sinned in that I have betrayed the innocent blood." Then, broken in heart and broken in hope, he hurried to hurl himself out of the world. Jesus lost Judas for the life that now is in that he ceased to love and trust him.

But what of the final destiny of Judas? Here the Bible is beautifully and tenderly reticent. Peter says of him simply that he went to his own place. That is delicately expressed. And yet how awful it is! If we look at it with open eyes, we cannot but feel that we are gazing into the very pits of hell. His own place— what kind of place would that be? It would be a place where traitors would fit in. It would be a place where one whose love had changed to hate would feel at home. And the words of Jesus only add to the blackness of that abode when he says with tender sorrow, "Good were it for that man if he had never been born." So far as our dim eyes can see the first destiny of Judas seems to be one without hope.

And the saddest part of all this grim tragedy, I think, is the needlessness of it. It was awful for Judas to change from a friend of Jesus to an enemy. It was awful for him to betray his Lord with a kiss. But, if possible, there was something that grieved our

Lord even more: that was his refusal, when he realized the tragic wreck he had made of his life, to throw himself on the mercy of Jesus and receive his forgiveness. Peter did, through cowardice, a deed almost as dastardly as that of Judas. But, with bitter tears, he turned again to him whom he had so greatly wronged. And Jesus could hardly wait to get the door of his tomb open on Easter morning before he said, "Go, tell my disciples and Peter." But Judas trusted in a hangman's noose more than in the amazing love of his betrayed Friend. That was his ruin. If he had only dared to come back as Peter did, it might have been written in the record, "Go, tell my disciples and Judas." And the blackest name of all history would have to-day been a monument of divine grace.

XV

PRAYING FOR OUR JOY

*"These things I speak in the world,
that they might have my joy fulfilled in themselves."*
JOHN 17: 13

I

THE FIRST FACT THAT STRIKES US IN THIS TEXT is the claim of Jesus to the possession of joy. He speaks not of the joy that was his in the morning-tide of life before he set out on his seemingly impossible mission. He is not looking back to the joy that was his in the early days of his ministry when eager and enthusiastic multitudes thronged about him. He speaks of joy as a present possession. Though he is even now under the shadow of the cross, though death is blowing its chill breath in his face, though his whole life now seems to be falling in ruins about him, he is yet able to look at it all with quiet eyes. The song in his heart is not hushed. The joy that has character-ized all his yesterdays is his still. And what a deep and satisfying joy that was! I am convinced that the gladdest heart that ever beat in a human bosom was that of Jesus. I am sure that the sunniest face that ever looked out upon this world was his face.

To be convinced of this, it is only necessary to turn again the pages that record his sayings. When he gives us a picture of a genuine Christian, as he does in the fifth chapter of St. Matthew, he is really speaking out of his own experience. He lived the Beatitudes before he spoke them. "Oh, the blessedness," he exclaims, "of those that mourn. Oh, the happiness, the joy of the meek, of the merciful, of the pure in heart. Oh, the joy of those who are persuaded for righteousness' sake!" He calls on all such to rejoice and be exceeding glad. And we may be sure that the joy that he offers and urges upon others was a rich possession of his own life.

Then, there is another expression that was a great favorite of his—that is, "Be of good cheer!" Again and again, he summons hopeless and sorrowing souls to lift up their hearts in joyful expectancy. One day four friends brought to him a man of whom sin had made a wreck. But Jesus saw vast possibilities in this bit of shattered human earthenware. Therefore he said, "Be of good cheer; thy sins are forgiven thee." Again on a black night of tempest, when his friends were fighting for their lives upon a storm-tossed sea, he called to them this same bracing word, "Be of good cheer." And here in this upper room, he has just said to them with steady voice and serene face, "In this world ye shall have tribulation: but be of good cheer;

I have overcome the world." And again we may be sure that the cheer that he was constantly offering to others was an abiding possession of his own heart.

In fact, as we read between the lines, we cannot fail to see that the gladness of Jesus was an offense to certain souls who looked upon religion as a stern something that takes the joy out of the life that now is. It was easy for them to believe that John the Baptist was a deeply religious man. He wore a camel's-hair shirt. He shunned all social functions. He lived upon a diet of locusts and wild honey. Certainly he was religious. But this Jesus, this young rabbi, who was constantly going out to dinner, who attended every banquet to which he was invited, who was a capital mixer, he could not be very religious. He was entirely too joyous. He was too much of a friend of publicans and sinners. He was, therefore, not a saint, but a mere gluttonous man, and a winebibber. Therefore, they flung away from him in disgust. But, if he alienated some by his too great joy, he drew others to him. There were those, then, as there are those to-day, who were short on joy. They found life a bit of a dreary winter. And when Jesus came with springtime in his heart, they pressed about him to learn his secret.

Of course, in asserting that Jesus was the most joyous of men, we are not denying that he was also a man of sorrows and acquainted with grief. Being the kind of man he was, he could not live in a world like ours without suffering. He was constantly bleeding

through the wounds of others. He was constantly
weeping through their tears. He was constantly stag-
gering under the weight of their heavy burdens. The
tragedies that dashed their hopes and broke their hearts
left their scars upon his own soul. But, in spite of
this—yes, and because of this—he was the most gladsome of men. Therefore, when he kneels to pray
among these sorrowing friends of his, he does not give
way to anguish. He does not say how much heavier
his own load is than theirs. He rather speaks of an
abiding joy, whose song is not hushed even in the presence of the tragedy of the cross.

II

The second fact that Jesus teaches us in this text is
his longing that the joy that is his may be ours. This
is most natural. How strange it would be if it were
the will of our Lord that his children be gloomy and
morose and sour! Yet Christianity has had to battle
against that conception through all the centuries. There
have always been those who seemed to fancy that the
Lord desired their wretchedness, and that the more
miserable they were, the more pleasing they were to
God. There are those even now who are desperately
afraid of anything that gives pleasure, forgetting that
no joy can be sinful unless it is sinful joy. Jesus is
so eager for us to be glad that when he prays this last
prayer, he requests that the joy that is his may be ours.

1. He desires that we be joyous because he loves us.

It is easy for us to understand that if we love. How many things we do for our children, not because they are absolutely necessary, but because we desire to make them glad. A man called to see me a few weeks before Christmas with a story that was a bit out of the ordinary. "I am working here," he said, "but I am making almost nothing. I can miss a few meals without hurt, but Christmas is at hand, and I have nothing with which to buy toys for my children. They have been writing letters to Santa Claus, and looking forward with such eagerness that it breaks my heart to disappoint them." And that man put his face in his two big, rugged hands and sobbed. He was not weeping because his children were hungry or cold, but because he was afraid that he was going to have to rob them of the joy of Christmas. And Jesus says, "If you, being evil, know how to give good gifts unto your children, how much more shall your Father in heaven give good things, things that make for joy, to them that ask him?" Jesus, then, desires our joy because he loves us.

2. He is eager for us to be joyful because joy is a great safeguard against temptation. Nature abhors a vacuum. If your heart is empty of joy, you are likely to entertain almost any kind of guest. But, if you have a full heart, then undesirable guests will knock at your door in vain. I sat reading last night, though black night was shrouding all my side of the world. But it could not get into the room where I was, be-

cause that room was full of light. And the moral
night that encircles us can be excluded by the inner
light that comes from our sharing the joy of our Lord.

This is a day when marriage ties have little binding
power, when husbands and wives fling away from each
other on the least provocation. But, there are those still
who come down to old age unspotted by illicit loves.
The tragic triangles that wreck so many other relation-
ships are to them unknown. Who are these that make
poetry out of the marriage relationship instead of soiled
and sordid prose? They are the husbands and wives
who find their joy in each other. I know a husband
to-day who still finds his wife the most delightful companion in all the world, and I think I know a wife who
has that same feeling about her husband. And this
joy, each in the other, makes the marriage relationship
safe. And just so, our possession of the joy of the
Lord makes us proof against the temptations of the
world.

3. Then, Jesus desires that we be joyous because the
joy of the Lord is our strength for the winning of our
fellows. I wonder if anybody was ever won to Christ
by a soured and joyless disciple? Do you remember
the testimony of the Elder Son in Jesus' immortal
story? It runs like this: "Lo, these many years do I
serve thee, neither transgressed I at any time thy commandment: and yet thou never gavest me a kid, that
I might make merry with my friends." How disappointing! And yet there are multitudes in the Church

to-day whose experiences are quite as lean and mean as that. By their indifference to the things of the spirit, by their long faces, by the care that looks out from their tired eyes, they say, "Though I belong to the Church, though I have been a more or less active member for five, ten, or twenty years, it has all been a songless and joyless affair. I have lived on a starvation diet, having never had as much as a kid with which to make merry with my friends."

Do you suppose that, after this Elder Son gave his testimony as to how badly he had been treated by his father, anybody came to him desiring to know his secret? Do you suppose that anybody asked an introduction to that penurious father? If you are constantly grouching, if you are forever complaining of the shabby way in which the Lord is treating you, do you think that anybody will desire to meet your Master? Not in a whole lifetime. But if you proclaim, by the joy that rings in your voice and looks out from your eyes, the goodness of God, if you have a song in your soul that all the discords of the world cannot hush, if you have the flowers of love and joy blooming in the garden of your heart, somebody is going to want to know your secret. Souls that are short on joy will gather about you just as the bees gather about a honeysuckle vine that has been kissed into beauty and fragrance by the springtime. The joy of the Lord is our strength for winning others.

III

But, how are we to come into the possession of joy? How may we know the joy that belonged to Jesus?

Let me mention first one or two roads by which we cannot arrive. We can never find real joy by getting into an ideal situation. In the first place, I do not know of anybody whose situation is entirely ideal. There is always something wanting. Of course there are many who face the fact that they are a bit poverty-stricken in joy at present, but they are going to be rich in the future. You are not very happy now as a student, but that will all be remedied when you get out of school. You are not very joyous now, but you will be as soon as you get married. As a husband or wife, you are far from being happy, but your joy will be full when you get a divorce. Some are going to be happy when the mortgage is paid; some, when they get back to work once more; some, when they recover their health. But all these as sources of abiding joy are disappointing.

> "Joy is the fruit that will not grow
>   On nature's barren soil.
> All we can boast, till Christ we know,
>   Is vanity and toil."

Nor are we going to find joy by seeking it as an end in itself. There are some treasures that we find more readily by taking the indirect way than the direct. Take sleep, for instance. I went to a certain town some years ago where I was to fill an important engagement. I

went to the hotel, but the pastor in whose church I was
to speak came, declaring that he had assigned me to one
of the loveliest homes of the city, and that the people
would be disappointed if I did not come. I was over-
persuaded, and went to this lovely home. There I
found myself with a roommate who tipped the scales at
near three hundred. He slept in the valley, and I
watched on the hill. Knowing how important it was
that I should sleep, I got in an immense hurry. But
the faster I ran, the more fleet-footed was sleep. It
was a little after the clock struck four when I gave
over the chase and slipped away into oblivion.

Now, joy is just as elusive when we say to ourselves: "Go to, now, I am going to be happy!" It is
Stanley Jones, I think, who tells of a lad whose mother
took him to a circus. The little fellow showed a surprising lack of interest. At last the indignant mother
took him in hand and shook him severely, and ex-
claimed: "You enjoy yourself now; I brought you
here to have a good time." We do not find joy by seeking it. We rather find the opposite. If I were to go
out to find the most weary and bored and wretched
souls in this city to-day, I should know exactly where
to go. I should go to the men and women who have
nothing to do, seven days in the week, but to amuse
themselves. The most utterly joyless people I know
are people who make it their business to seek for joy—
morning, noon, and night.

How, then, shall we find joy? How did Jesus find it?

1. Jesus was joyful because of his profound and abiding confidence in God. He was always sure of his Father's love and care. The feverish and fear-filled lives of the people about him were a constant source of amazement. Their worries filled him with pained surprise. How could they be so frightened and joyless in a God-ordered world? "Consider the lilies of the field," he exclaims, "how they grow; they toil not, neither do they spin: and yet I say unto you, That even Solomon in all his glory was not arrayed like one of these. Wherefore, if God so clothe the grass of the field, which to-day is, and to-morrow is cast into the oven, shall he not much more clothe you, O ye of little faith?" Jesus lived always in the joy of an unbounded confidence in God. Even on the cross, his enemies flung at him this accusation: "He trusted in God." And those who share his faith will also share his joy.

2. A second source of the joy of Jesus was his confidence in men. He trusted men with a fullness that amazes us to this day. This does not mean, of course, that he shut his eyes to the tragedy of man's sin. He saw that grim tragedy more clearly than any other that ever lived. He not only saw the tragedy of man's sin, but all the sufferings that are born of that terrible tragedy. He never blinked the fact that men were lost. When he started his mission, he declared that the Son of Man had come to seek and to save that which is lost.

He constantly affirmed that his gospel is a gospel for sinners, and for sinners only. He knew, through his own first-hand experiences, the depths to which sin could sink men. One of his closest friends denied him, and swore that he had never known him. Another betrayed him with a kiss and flung him into the hands of ruthless enemies that crucified him.

But, though men killed his body, they could never kill his faith. If Jesus faced the fact of man's sin, he was equally sure of his possible sainthood. One day, when he went to Jericho, he became the guest of a certain renegade named Zaccheus. This man was perhaps the worst hated man in the city. Naturally his conduct stirred hot antagonism in the hearts of the respectable people. But Jesus justified himself by saying, "He also is the son of Abraham." By this he meant not simply that this outcast publican was a descendant of Abraham; he rather meant that he had within him that moral and spiritual worth that made him akin to him who was the friend of God and the father of the faithful. This faith in men was naturally a source of great joy. In fact, we cannot be joyous without some bit of this confidence. If you trust nobody, you are wretched. Elijah was a strong and good man. But when he reached the conclusion that he had a monopoly in goodness, when he felt forced to say, "They have slain thy prophets . . . and I only I am left," he was ready to die. And no wonder! If you would find joy, you must not only trust in God, but also in man.

3. Finally, the joy of Jesus was the joy of perfect consecration to God. Every consecrated soul is a joyous soul. This we can assert with absolute conviction. This we can assert without any qualification. The man who is consecrated to God, whether he is popular or unpopular, whether men throw mud at him or throw bouquets at him, whether he lives in a palace or lives in a hovel, whether he is tortured by pain or is blessed by vigorous health, whether he toils in obscurity or with the spotlight of the world playing upon him, regardless of circumstances, the consecrated man is a joyous man. I am confident that there is not an exception in the wide world. Here, for instance, is a little group in the morningtide of the Church. They are coming home from a meeting that they have not attended from choice. But, in spite of this fact, there is a light in their eyes that thrills us after nineteen centuries. What is the matter? Have they been given some honorary degree? No, instead, they have been disgracefully beaten. "And they departed, rejoicing that they were counted worthy to suffer shame for his name."

If, then, every consecrated soul is joyous, what is the meaning of our lack of joy? Is it not here that we are not really consecrated? How many restless and disappointed and joyless people we have in our churches to-day! Why is it so? It is not because Jesus cannot do for us what he claims to do. It is not because the joy that was his is beyond our reach. It is because we are only half-hearted in our allegiance. We have failed

fully to surrender to him. We complain that we do
not have a sense of his presence, when the whole trouble is that we are not willing to go in the direction in
which he is going. "Follow me," said Jesus. And he
goes out to take the burdens of the world upon his
shoulders. He goes to needy children. He goes to desperate and lonely men and women. And if we set our
face in that direction, our paths and his will run together. We shall surely meet him. And the joy that
is his will be ours. For, if we share his consecration,
we shall certainly share his faith and his abounding
joy.

XVI

PRAYING FOR OUR SANCTIFICATION
"Sanctify them."
JOHN 17: 17

SANCTIFICATION IS A VERBAL COIN THAT HAS slipped out of circulation. We no longer use it in our daily conversations one with another. We never meet it in our newspapers or magazines or books of popular fiction. To the average man, it has no form nor comeliness. It simply means nothing at all. To others, it is a rather offensive word. It smacks of fanaticism. It is a red flag of controversy. It sets them to breathing out threatenings and slaughter. Then, to a few, it is still a living word, kept fresh and green by the dewdrops of a vital Christian experience.

I

"Sanctify them," Jesus prays. For what is he asking? I take it that he is not praying that we may reach a certain moral and spiritual height beyond which no further progress is possible. It is my conviction that we shall never attain such a height either in this life or in that which is to come. I am sure that we shall

always be able to sing with Tennyson, "Not in vain
the distance beckons. Forward, forward! let us range."
I am certain we can always shout with Paul, "Let us
press toward the mark for the prize." "We know not
what we shall be; but we know that, when he shall
appear, we shall be like him; for we shall see him as
he is." But even this likeness will not be perfect. We
shall go on becoming increasingly like him as we climb
one mountain height after another with him through
eternity.

Nor can we look on this as a calamity. It would
rather be a calamity should we be able to attain the
height of our possibilities at a single bound. Life
loses its tang when to-morrow offers no possibility of
progress. There is real reason in that old story that
when Alexander the Great had conquered the world,
he wept because there were no more worlds to conquer.
Well he might weep. In his early thirties he had
reached the mountain peak of his possibilities. At that
early hour he was standing upon the very apex of his
life, and there was no step that he could take that would
not be a downward step. There is little wonder, therefore, that he went away to drown his heartache by
drinking himself to death. But life may always thrill
for you and me if we walk with Christ. To us through
all eternity our best and finest adventures will always be
ahead of us.

What, then, is it to be sanctified? It is to be consecrated. It is to be fully surrendered to the will of

God. It is to seek first, always and everywhere, the Kingdom of God and his righteousness. We have seen men thus consecrated to their professions. We have seen them thus consecrated to business. There are men all about us who put their business first. This does not mean that they are always at the store or at the office. It does mean that whatever they do, they have an eye single to the success of their business. If they play golf, it is to fit them the better to attend to business. If they join a club or a fraternity, it is for the purpose of helping forward their business. If they entertain friends, that same purpose is supreme. Even when they join a church, as they sometimes do, their business interests are first. A gentleman came to me in another city some years ago, proposing to give my church a certain per cent of all his profit if I would advertise his wares from my pulpit. He was fully consecrated to his business.

Now, it is thus that we are to be consecrated to God. Our pleasures and our pastimes are to have as their goal that we may serve him the better. Our business is not to be an end in itself, but a means to an end. Whether we eat or drink, or whatever we do, we are to do all to the glory of God. When business and the will of God clash for the man who puts business first, then the will of God must stand aside. And that, the will of God has to do over and over again. But, for the man who puts God first, when business, or pleasure, or inclination clash with his will, then all these must stand aside. To be sanctified, to be consecrated, is to bring every word and thought and deed, every decision, up before this high test, "Will it please God?"

Now, the man who is thus consecrated is reckoned throughout the Scriptures as perfect. Christian perfection is not perfect attainment. It is not faultlessness. It is whole-heartedness. Noah, for instance, is spoken of as a perfect man, and yet, every Sunday school child can point out his faults. Paul prayed for his converts after this fashion: "And the very God of peace sanctify you wholly; and I pray God your whole spirit and soul and body be preserved blameless unto the coming of our Lord Jesus Christ." Notice what the great apostle counts upon as following upon the heels of their entire santification. It is not faultlessness, but blamelessness. We shall always blunder more or less. We shall always be faulty as long as we live in this world. But in spite of our faults, we may yet be blameless.

Years ago, when I was a teacher, there was a girl among my pupils who was a bit of a half-wit. Now, it so happened that this dull girl was one of my devoted admirers. (I do not mention that, however, as a mark of her dullness.) One day she slipped up behind me, and anointed me with a whole bottle of cheap perfume. As a result I had to hurry home and change my clothing. The service she rendered was a very faulty service. There was a sense in which it did far more harm than good. Yet, it was beautifully blameless, because it was actuated by such a lovely motive. And our services are oftentimes quite as faulty; but if they are wrought under the impulse of a loving heart, they are blameless and beautiful in the eyes of our Lord. Both they and ourselves are reckoned as perfect.

II

Notice next how Jesus seeks to bring about our sanctification. He believes that entire surrender to the will of God is a possibility for every one of us. But how does he hope to bring us to that high goal?

1. By the santification of himself. "For their sakes I sanctify myself, that they also may be sanctified." Jesus was constantly surrendering himself to the will of God. It was this consecration that lay back of his incarnation. It was because of this that the Word was made flesh and dwelt among us. It was his complete consecration to the will of God that sent him to the task of world-redemption. It was this consecration that led him to break with the religious leaders of his day. It was this consecration that caused him to suffer death upon the cross. He died rather than fail in the slightest degree to do the will of God. And it was his faith that through his own consecration we should be led to the consecration of ourselves. And there is no denying the fact that the sanctification of himself has been the most compelling of all motives for us to concentrate ourselves. Of course there are those who have resisted and who resist still. But countless millions

213

have responded. Lifted up from the earth, he has drawn all men unto himself.

Now consecration for the sake of others always has something unspeakably beautiful about it. And we have all known something of it in the lives of those closest to us. That is the reason we are here this morning. I was re-reading recently the tragic story of the Titanic. I was struck especially by the conduct of Mrs. Isadore Strauss, who was on board with her husband. She was offered a place in one of the lifeboats. She started to take it; but when she found that her husband could not go with her, she immediately stepped back, saying, "We have been together for many years; where you go, I go." And she consecrated herself in order to die with him. On a backwoods farm in Tennessee, I knew a father and mother whose seemingly homely lives were a halo of surpassing beauty because they were constantly sanctifying themselves for the sake of their children. They were parting with life that they might enable their children to see more than they had seen, and to be more than they had been.

2. Not only does Jesus sanctify himself that we might be sanctified, but he prays for our sanctification. Now, prayer is the mightiest weapon that human hands can wield. But it is only mighty in the hands of the consecrated. It is the effectual fervent prayer of a righteous man that availeth much. Half-hearted saints cannot pray. "If I regard iniquity in my heart, God will not hear me." It is only when our prayers are

backed by our lives that they become mighty. To pray
for the sanctification of our fellows, and then do naked
nothing to bring that consummation to pass, is little
short of mockery. The measure of the might of our
prayers is the thoroughness of our consecration. If
we are entirely devoted to the will of God, our prayers
will be all but omnipotent, "Whatsoever we ask, we receive of him, because we keep his commandments and
do the things that are pleasing in his sight."

III

Why does Jesus seek our sanctification?

1. He does so because there is no salvation without
it. There are those who look upon sanctification as a
second work of grace, far higher than regeneration.
But without our sanctification, which means nothing
more than our entire surrender, there can be no regeneration. There can be no knowing God at all. If you
were instructing a penitent, what particular duty would
you tell him that God would permit him to neglect?
What particular sin would you tell him that God would
allow him to continue to practice? None at all. We
all know that God has no plan of salvation for an unsurrendered heart. "If any man willeth to do his will,
he shall know." He shall come to spiritual certainty.
In the faces of all others, the door is shut.

Here, for example, are two men who were brought
under the spell of Jesus. One of them was the Rich
Young Ruler. He met the Master and was fascinated

by him. But our Lord put his finger upon the chain that bound him and, desiring to set him free, said, "Go thy way, sell whatsoever thou hast, and give to the poor: and come, follow me." But the demand was heavier than he was willing to meet. Therefore, we read that he went away. Jesus did not drive him away. He did not put his hands upon his two shoulders and turn him about and push him away. He went away, and going, he missed Eternal Life; missed it, not because Jesus did not love him, but because he refused to surrender. He would not consecrate himself.

Paul's situation was far more difficult than that of the Rich Young Ruler. He was the hope of his church, the leader of the opposition to the cause of Christianity. But on the way from Jerusalem to Damascus, he had a vision of Jesus that prostrated him in the dust. He went away from that experience to become one of the world's greatest saints, and its mightiest missionary. But how was this vision of Jesus able to do this for Paul? There was no force in it. Paul might have gone from the white brightness of that vision into a deeper darkness. Many a man has done so. That which changed Paul from a sinner into a saint, from a persecutor into a prophet, was his personal surrender. He puts the whole secret in this great sentence: "Whereupon O king Agrippa, I was not disobedient unto the heavenly vision." Jesus, therefore, longs for our sanctification, because without it we can never come to spiritual certainty.

2. Not only is sanctification necessary if we are to come to know God, but it is necessary if we are to continue in fellowship with him. Jesus could enjoy this fellowship in no other way. "He that hath sent me is with me. The Father hath not left me alone, because I do always the things that please him." Paul died to himself out on the Damascus road that day, and that brought him into fellowship with his Lord. But that one death was not enough. In order to continue in that fellowship, he had to die daily. Every morning he died afresh to the call of the world. Every day he died anew to sin and to self.

Now, it is this daily dying that makes possible our growth in grace. To become a Christian at all, it is necessary to make an unconditional surrender. But if we are to be growing Christians, we are sure to discover day by day new sacrifices that we ought to make, new lands that we ought to possess. Speaking out of my own personal experience, the most difficult surrenders that I have had to make were not those that I made at the time of my conversion. They have been those along the way. But there must be this day by day obedience, or we lose the fellowship of our Lord. "Lo, I am with you always," Jesus declares. But this is only possible if we walk with him to disciple the nations. If we are not constantly making his purpose our purposes, his battles our battles, we cannot enjoy his fellowship.

3. Finally, he longs for our sanctification, because it is thus, and only thus, that we can come to our fullest

possibilities of life and power. It is evident that Jesus
never intended that we should carry on in energy of
the flesh. The tasks to which he sets us are far too big.
Therefore, he has promised us a power beyond the
human. "Ye shall receive power, after that the Holy
Spirit is come upon you." It is through the power of
the Spirit that we are to witness for him. This Spirit
makes possible our witness through our transformed
personalities. This was the witness of Peter and John,
when their foes were compelled to take knowledge of
them that they had been with Jesus. We are to witness
also through our spoken testimony. He has promised
a mouth and a wisdom that men cannot gainsay nor
resist. It is through such testimony that we can win.
And the victory is possible in no other way.

Jesus himself won through this power. When
Luke undertakes to account for his marvelous spiritual
adequacy, he does not do so by affirming that he was
divine. Of course Luke believed in the unique deity
of Jesus. But he also believed that he was as completely human as we are, that he lived his life under
exactly the same limitations that we live ours. Therefore, the fact that he went about doing good was due,
not to his deity, but to the fact that God anointed him
with the Holy Spirit and with power. And when Jesus
accounts for himself, he speaks to the same purpose.
"The Spirit of the Lord is upon me, because he hath
anointed me to preach the gospel to the poor; he hath

sent me to heal the broken-hearted, to preach deliverance to the captives, and recovering of sight to the blind, to set at liberty them that are bruised." And if the Holy Spirit was necessary for Jesus, surely he is necessary for you and me. And he may be ours by our becoming his. "And we are his witnesses of these things; and so is also the Holy Spirit, whom God hath given to them that obey him." Thus, it is evident that our personal salvation, our continuous fellowship with God, our spiritual power, are all conditioned upon our sanctification, our whole-hearted surrender to God.

IV

Now, it ought to be enough for us who call Jesus Lord to know that he longs for our sanctification. Seeing that he has paid the price of his own sanctification for ourselves, we surely ought to sanctify ourselves. We ought to listen anew to the words of Paul as he writes, "I beseech you therefore, brethren, by the mercies of God, that ye present your bodies a living sacrifice, holy, acceptable unto God, which is your reasonable service." But, strange to say, many of us hold back. Many of us continue half-hearted. We therefore continue in the possession of an experience that satisfies neither God nor man. I have known many half-hearted Christians. But I have never known one to rejoice over his failure fully to consecrate himself to God.

On the other hand, I have never known a single
fully surrendered man that did not rejoice that he had
made that surrender, however great its cost. It cost
Stephen his life. But the joy of his heart was so full
that those who saw his face saw it as the face of an
angel. It was my privilege a few years ago to hear a
Quaker missionary who had been for fourteen years
in the long-grass country of Africa. The tribe that he
served was one of the most barbarous. They wore no
shred of clothing. At first he was not wanted. Then,
too, he had to pick up their language word by word,
slowly and painfully. There was one word that they
did not seem to have in their vocabulary at all, and that
was the word "save." But one night, after three years
of working and waiting, they were sitting about the
camp fire, discussing the events of the day. The old
chief told that, as he was coming through the brush
that day a man-eating lion got after him, and a certain
slave of his saved him.

And this missionary sprang to his feet and put his
hand upon the black man's shoulder and said, "That
is what I have been trying to tell you that the man
Christ Jesus did for you." And that dark face lighted
with a light that was never seen on land or sea. And
then the missionary added this amazing testimony.
He said: "I have had forty-two cases of African
fever. I have been much of the time without a companion. For fourteen months I have had to live on
ants, rhinocerous meat, and curded milk. But know-

ing all that it would mean of loneliness and suffering, I would gladly go through it all again to get to see that one black face to light up by the camp fire as it did that night." "Sanctify them," Jesus prays. And in so praying he is seeking our highest possibilities. Let us make possible that prayer by giving ourselves wholly to God.